# Political Philosophers

Quick and Concise

# Political Philosophers

**Deboshruti Roychowdhury**

hachette INDIA

First published in 2025 by Hachette India
(Registered name: Hachette Book Publishing India Pvt. Ltd)
An Hachette UK company
www.hachetteindia.com

1



ISBN: 978-93-5731-685-9

Hachette Book Publishing India Pvt. Ltd
4th & 5th Floors, Corporate Centre
Plot No. 94, Sector 44, Gurugram – 122003, India

Typeset in Athelas 11/15
by InoSoft Systems

Printed and bound in India
by Thomson Press India Ltd.

MIX
Paper | Supporting responsible forestry
FSC® C010615

# CONTENTS


1. Transition from Ancient to Modern Philosophy: A Comprehensive History 1
2. Philosophy in Action: Exploring Ideas that Shaped Society 14
3. Defining Moments in Philosophy: Ideas that Changed the World 18
4. The Evolution of Political Philosophy: From Ancient Foundations to Renaissance Reforms 23
5. The Thinkers Who Shaped Political Philosophy 36
    - Socrates: The Father of Philosophy 37
    - Plato: The Visionary of Idealism 44
    - Aristotle: The Philosopher of Practical Wisdom 52
    - Montesquieu: The Architect of Political Freedom and the Separation of Powers 61
    - Voltaire: The Advocate of Freedom, Tolerance and Reason 73
    - Jean-Jacques Rousseau: The Champion of Democracy and the Social Contract 81

- Immanuel Kant: The Philosopher of Duty and Universal Ethics 90
- Georg Wilhelm Friedrich Hegel: The Philosopher of History and Reality 97
- John Stuart Mill: The Advocate for Liberty and Utilitarianism 108
- Karl Marx: The Revolutionary Thinker of Class Struggle and Communism 120
- Max Weber: The Sociologist Who Bridged Philosophy and Political Theory 132
- Friedrich Nietzsche: The Philosopher of Individualism and the Will to Power 142
- John Locke: The Father of Liberalism 152
- Dr B.R. Ambedkar: The Architect of Modern Indian Democracy 159
- Hannah Arendt: The Thinker of Totalitarianism, Power and Freedom 167
- Emma Goldman: The Voice of Anarchism and Revolutionary Thought 175
- John Rawls: Architect of Modern Political Justice 184

6. A Call to Engage: Political Philosophy as a Living Conversation 195

# I

# TRANSITION FROM ANCIENT TO MODERN PHILOSOPHY

## *A Comprehensive History*

### INTRODUCTION: THE ENDURING JOURNEY OF PHILOSOPHICAL INQUIRY

Philosophy has served as humanity's guiding compass across the ages, helping us explore life's most profound questions – about the nature of existence, knowledge, morality and the cosmos itself. This narrative journeys through the ages, from the earliest musings of ancient civilization to the rich and intricate debates of the modern world. The book further illustrates how each epoch not only mirrors the societal values of its time but also profoundly shapes them, leaving its imprint on human history.

Philosophy has always evolved as the world did, deeply influenced by the sociopolitical and religious transformations of its time. The democratic experiments of ancient Greece gave rise to groundbreaking ideas about governance and ethics, while the vast empires of the Hellenistic era enriched philosophical thought through new cultural exchanges. During the medieval period, philosophical inquiries were inspired by religion and the divine. Then came the Renaissance, a humanist revival that rekindled curiosities about individuality and human potential. These transitions shaped the trajectory of human thought through each era, emphasizing philosophy's dual role as both a reflection of and a catalyst for change.

## 1. ANCIENT PHILOSOPHY (c. 600 BCE–323 BCE): PHILOSOPHY IN THE AGE OF THE POLIS

Humanity's first steps into rational inquiry or the story of ancient philosophy began in the city-states of Greece, particularly Athens, during a period marked by political experimentation and cultural flourishing. This era saw a pivotal shift from explaining the world through mythological tales to exploring it through reason and observation.

### The Birth of the Polis: A Sociopolitical Context

The Greek city-state, or polis, emerged as the central unit of political and social life during this period. Unlike the sprawling empires of Egypt or Mesopotamia, the Greek polis was small, autonomous and centred on civic participation. In Athens, the development of early democratic structures allowed for open debate and intellectual exchange, providing fertile ground for philosophical thought to flourish.

The Peloponnesian War (431–404 BCE) between Athens and Sparta brought political turmoil that forced thinkers to grapple with deep philosophical questions about justice, governance and the nature of power. Philosophers like Socrates (469–399 BCE), who is often seen as the father of Western philosophy, challenged Athenians with his scrutinizing questions to examine their values and actions critically.

### Religion and the Shift to Rational Inquiry

While Greek society remained deeply religious, this era witnessed a gradual shift from reliance on divine explanations to rational reason. Early philosophers like Thales of Miletus (c. 624–546 BCE) began to explore natural causes for phenomena like earthquakes and eclipses, setting a precedent for observation and logic-based inquiry. This marked the birth of a tradition that sought balance in respect for myth and commitment to rationality.

### The Transition to the Hellenistic Period

The death of Alexander the Great in 323 BCE marked the end of the classical era. His conquests unified the Greek world but also introduced new cultural exchanges, dissolving the polis as the centre of political and intellectual life. This shift set the stage for a new philosophical focus – from communal questions of politics and society to personal ethics and emotional resilience. The seeds sown during this time would shape philosophical thought for centuries to come.

## 2. THE HELLENISTIC PERIOD (c. 323 BCE–31 BCE): PHILOSOPHY IN AN ERA OF EMPIRE

The Hellenistic period was a time of transformation, defined by the fragmentation of Alexander's empire and the rise of vast, multi-ethnic kingdoms. Philosophy, too, evolved to meet the challenges of the new sociopolitical realities, focusing on personal well-being and coping strategies for individuals navigating an increasingly cosmopolitan and unstable world.

**Political Instability and Cultural Exchange**

The dissolution of Alexander's empire gave rise to successor states, such as the Seleucid, Ptolemaic and Antigonid kingdoms. These new realms blended Greek culture with Persian, Egyptian and Indian traditions. This cross-cultural exchange enriched philosophical discourse further, introducing new ideas about fate, morality and the divine.

At the same time, the loss of civic autonomy in the Greek city-states created a sense of alienation. Philosophical schools stepped in to address this feeling of disconnection from traditional communal identities. Stoicism, founded by Zeno of Citium (c. 334–262 BCE), emphasized living in harmony with nature and accepting life's challenges with equanimity. Epicureanism, led by Epicurus (341–270 BCE), advocated for simple pleasures, freedom from fear and the avoidance of pain, offering a blueprint for personal tranquility in turbulent times.

**Intellectual Hubs and Knowledge Preservation**

The Hellenistic era was also a golden age for learning. Centres like the Library of Alexandria, established in the early third century BCE under Ptolemy I, became repositories of knowledge and innovation. This institution symbolized the era's commitment to preserving and expanding human knowledge, serving as a bridge between the classical world and later intellectual traditions.

### Transition to the Roman Era

The Roman conquest of Greece in 146 BCE brought Hellenistic philosophy into the heart of Roman culture. Roman thinkers adapted Greek ideas to address practical concerns such as governance and law and the management of empire. This fusion of philosophical and pragmatic thought paved the way for the integration of philosophical and religious traditions in the medieval period.

## 3. MEDIEVAL PHILOSOPHY (c. 500 CE–1500 CE): FAITH, REASON AND THE LEGACY OF EMPIRE

The fall of the Western Roman Empire in 476 CE ushered in the medieval period, an era when classical philosophy became deeply intertwined with Christian and Islamic theology.

### The Role of Religion

Faith was central to medieval life, and philosophical inquiry was often directed towards theological questions. St. Augustine (354–430 CE) bridged the classical and medieval worlds, blending Platonic thought with Christian doctrine in his seminal works like *The City of God*, which presented history as a struggle between divine and earthly realms.

The Islamic Golden Age (8th–13th centuries) was another key contributor to medieval thought. Scholars like Avicenna (980–1037 CE) and Averroës (1126–1198 CE) preserved and expanded on Aristotelian philosophy, introducing them to new audiences and blending them with Islamic theology. Their efforts not only enriched Islamic intellectual traditions but also influenced European scholasticism.

### The Sociopolitical Landscape

Medieval philosophy reflected the hierarchical structure of feudal society, where kings, nobles and the Church wielded authority. Monasteries and universities became centres of learning, fostering the development of scholastic methods that emphasized logical analysis and debate.

However, the Crusades (1095–1291) brought increased contact between Europe and the Islamic culture, introducing new knowledge and perspectives. These exchanges enriched European intellectual life, challenging thinkers to integrate diverse ideas into their own frameworks.

### Transition to the Renaissance

The rediscovery of classical texts and the weakening of feudal structures set the stage for the Renaissance. As feudal structures weakened, trade and urbanization created a more secular intellectual climate, challenging the dominance of religious authority and paving the way for humanism. The focus moved from divine matters to the potential and achievements of humanity, marking a turning point in the history of philosophy.

## 4. THE RENAISSANCE (c. 1400 CE–1600 CE): THE REVIVAL OF HUMANISM

The Renaissance, or 'rebirth', was a transformative period of renewed interest in classical antiquity and a celebration of human potential. This era, marked by cultural, social and intellectual change, was shaped by sociopolitical transformations, technological innovations and a growing emphasis on individual agency.

## The Black Death and Social Change

The devastating pandemic, the Black Death (1347–51), swept through Europe, claiming the lives of an estimated 25–30 million people, nearly a third of the continent's population. This catastrophe weakened feudal structures, leading to labour shortages and increasing social mobility. Surviving workers and peasants began to demand better wages and working conditions. The Church's inability to prevent or explain the plague weakened its authority, creating a fertile ground for intellectual and cultural renewal, setting the stage for the Renaissance.

## Humanism and the Rediscovery of Antiquity

At the heart of the Renaissance was humanism, a cultural and intellectual movement that sought to revive the classical ideals of ancient Greece and Rome. At its core, humanism celebrates dignity, worth and the potential of the individual. This marked a significant shift from the medieval focus on divine authority and collective salvation to an exploration of human achievements, capacities and responsibilities.

Key social figures like Petrarch (1304–74), often called the 'Father of Humanism', advocated the study of the humanities–grammar, rhetoric, poetry, history and moral philosophy. These disciplines, collectively known as studia humanitatis, were believed to cultivate virtue and wisdom. Humanists encouraged a return to classical texts to extract moral and practical lessons that could guide contemporary life.

The rediscovery of antiquity was fuelled by several factors. Scholars who fled during the fall of Constantinople in 1453 brought with them Greek manuscripts that had been lost to the Latin West for centuries. These texts, combined with the invention of the printing press by Johannes Gutenberg, in 1440, made classical knowledge more widely accessible. This intellectual revival wasn't just about admiring the past but about applying its lessons to address contemporary challenges.

Humanism transformed education, politics and art. Niccolò Machiavelli (1469–1527) applied classical realism in his analysis of power in *The Prince* while artists like Michelangelo and Leonardo da Vinci captured human form and emotion with unprecedented depth, reflecting the humanist celebration of human potential.

**Sociopolitical Shifts and the Rise of Individual Agency**

The Renaissance reshaped Europe's social and political landscape. The feudal system, which had dominated the medieval period, began to weaken due to factors like the Black Death, which had decimated populations and disrupted traditional hierarchies. Labour shortages allowed peasants and artisans to demand better wages and working conditions, fostering a sense of individual empowerment.

Urbanization and the rise of powerful city-states like Florence, Venice, and Milan created new opportunities for commerce, culture and governance. These city-states were often ruled by merchant families, such as the Medici in Florence, who used their wealth to patronize artists and intellectuals. This shift from feudal lordships to urban centres of power marked a transition towards more dynamic and competitive political systems.

The Renaissance also saw the emergence of centralized monarchies in countries like France, Spain and England.

These monarchies sought to consolidate power, often clashing with the Catholic Church. This growing tension between secular and religious authorities reflected broader shifts in societal values as individuals and communities began to assert their autonomy in both political and spiritual matters.

### The Role of Religion in the Renaissance

Though often associated with secular achievements, the Renaissance was deeply intertwined with religion. The Catholic Church remained a dominant institution, funding much of the art and architecture of the period. Michelangelo's Sistine Chapel and Raphael's Vatican frescoes, for example, were commissioned by the papacy and reflected religious themes infused with humanist ideals, emphasizing the beauty and potential of creation.

However, the Church's authority faced growing challenges. The Protestant Reformation, initiated by Martin Luther (1483–1546) in 1517, marked a turning point in religious thought. Luther's *Ninety-five Theses*, critiquing Church practices like the sale of indulgences and other corrupt customs, sparked a religious upheaval that divided Europe into Catholic and Protestant regions. This shift or the Reformation aligned with the humanist ideals of personal agency and emphasized the individual's direct relationship with god, challenging the Church's mediatory role.

In response, the Catholic Church launched the Counter-Reformation, reaffirming its doctrines and commissioning works of art to inspire faith and devotion. Despite these efforts, the Reformation permanently altered the religious landscape of Europe, creating a more fragmented but pluralistic spiritual environment.

## Transition to the Enlightenment: The Path to Reason and Progress

The Renaissance's revival of classical learning and its celebration of human potential laid the groundwork for the Enlightenment, an intellectual movement that emerged in the seventeenth and eighteenth centuries. This transition was characterized by a shift from reliance on tradition and authority to an emphasis on reason, empirical evidence and progress.

Advances in science played a critical role in this shift. The works of Copernicus, Galileo and Kepler during the Renaissance challenged long-held beliefs about the cosmos, demonstrating that the Earth was not the centre of the universe. These discoveries not only transformed humanity's understanding of nature but also encouraged a spirit of inquiry that questioned all forms of established authority, including religious and political institutions. The Enlightenment philosophy expanded on Renaissance ideals, applying rationale to address questions of governance, ethics and human rights. Thinkers like John Locke (1632–1704) argued for natural rights and the social contract, laying the groundwork for modern democracy. Similarly, the Enlightenment's commitment to education and knowledge dissemination owed much to the humanist ideals of the Renaissance.

While the Renaissance celebrated individual achievements, the Enlightenment expanded this vision to include collective progress. The period's belief in human reason and potential, tempered by lessons from the Renaissance, laid the foundation for revolutionary changes in society, science and politics.

## 5. MODERN PHILOSOPHY (c. 1800 CE–PRESENT): A PLURALISTIC AND GLOBAL INQUIRY

Modern philosophy has been marked by diverse and complex inquiries, reflecting the sociopolitical upheavals, scientific advancements and cultural transformations of the past two centuries. This era gave rise to major philosophical movements that questioned human existence, the nature of knowledge and the structures of society through increasingly specialized and global lenses.

### The Sociopolitical Context of Modern Philosophy

The nineteenth and twentieth centuries witnessed unprecedented political and social change, shaped by the Industrial Revolution, the rise of nation-states, global conflicts and movements advocating democracy and human rights. Philosophical thought during this time often mirrored these upheavals, grappling with the implications of modernity, technological progress and the quest for individual autonomy.

Romanticism, emerging in the early nineteenth century, pushed back against industrialization, celebrating emotion, nature and the sublime. This movement was followed by existentialism in the mid-twentieth century, with thinkers like Søren Kierkegaard (1813–55) and later Jean-Paul Sartre (1905–80) exploring themes of alienation, existentialism, freedom and the search for meaning in an indifferent world. Their work resonated deeply with societies recovering from the devastation of two World Wars.

## The Analytic and Continental Traditions

Modern philosophy has been notably characterized by the split between analytic and continental traditions.

- The Analytic School: Thinkers like Bertrand Russell (1872–1970) and Ludwig Wittgenstein (1889–1951) focused on language, logic and scientific precision. Their work sought to clarify philosophical problems by analysing the structure of thought and communication, aligning closely with the methods of natural science.
- The Continental Tradition: Influenced by German idealism and phenomenology, this school explored human experience, culture and history. Idealists like Georg Wilhelm Friedrich Hegel (1770–1831), and later, existentialists and phenomenologists like Edmund Husserl (1859–1938) examined the interplay of subjective and collective realities, paving the way for existential and postmodern thought

These contrasting approaches reflect the growing complexity of philosophical inquiry as thinkers grappled with both universal and deeply contextual issues.

## Global Influences and Decolonial Thought

The twentieth century saw the rise of global and post-colonial perspectives in philosophy. Thinkers like Frantz Fanon (1925–61) and Gayatri Chakravorty Spivak (b. 1942) evaluated Western philosophical frameworks, highlighting the lived experiences of colonized peoples and the importance of decolonizing knowledge systems. Frantz Fanon critiqued the legacies of colonialism, exposing the psychological and cultural scars inflicted on colonized populations while Gayatri Spivak highlighted the silenced voices of the Global South, advocating for the deconstruction of Eurocentric frameworks.

These movements have enriched modern philosophy by challenging Eurocentric assumptions and integrating diverse cultural perspectives.

### The Transition to Postmodernism: Questioning Certainties

By the late twentieth century, postmodernism emerged as a critique of overarching narratives and universal truths. Thinkers like Michel Foucault (1926–84) and Jacques Derrida (1930–2004) deconstructed traditional categories of knowledge and power, revealing the fluid and constructed nature of reality.

This era reframed philosophy as a tool for questioning rather than defining, influencing disciplines such as literary theory, sociology and political science. Issues of gender, race and identity became central to philosophical discourse, reflecting the pluralistic and interconnected world of the modern era.

### The Ongoing Journey

Philosophy continues to evolve with the complexities of the twenty-first century, grappling with the ethical dilemmas posed by climate change, globalization, and more recently, artificial intelligence. Contemporary philosophy remains a dynamic field, enriched by its pluralistic roots and commitment to addressing the pressing questions of our time.

# 2

# PHILOSOPHY IN ACTION

## *Exploring Ideas that Shaped Society*

Philosophy is known to have shaped human thought, continuously adapting and evolving with changing society, politics and culture. The ideas of ancient, medieval and modern philosophers contributed to the bigger picture of political thought of every era. These philosophical ideas reflect the societies that birthed them while also altering the course of history as they moved forward.

Each philosopher, in their own way, responded to the world around them, either by challenging the status quo or offering new visions of governance, justice and the human condition.

### ANCIENT PHILOSOPHY

#### 1. Heraclitus and the River of Change

**Timeline:** Heraclitus of Ephesus (c. 540–480 BCE)

**Anecdote:** Heraclitus famously said, 'You cannot step into the same river twice,' which highlights the constant flux and ever-changing nature of life. He believed that everything is in perpetual motion and nothing remains the same.

**Context of the Quote:** Heraclitus compared life to a flowing river. Although the river looks constant, the water is always moving and changing. This metaphor reflects the transient nature of existence, where both us and the world around us is always transforming.

**Sociopolitical Significance:** At a time when Greek city-states were constantly changing, Heraclitus' philosophy mirrored the instability of political alliances and social systems. His focus on change suggested that nothing is permanent, a concept that helped people deal with the uncertainties and unpredictabilities of the time.

### 2. Plato and the Cave

**Timeline:** Plato (c. 428–348 BCE)

**Anecdote:** In *The Republic*, Plato describes a group of people who have been chained in a cave their whole lives, facing only a wall. They watch shadows cast by objects passing in front of a fire behind them, believing them to be reality. According to Plato, the shadows are the prisoners' reality, but they are not accurate representations of the real world.

**Sociopolitical Significance:** Plato used this allegory to show that through education, we can escape the 'cave' of ignorance and discover the actual truth. This story critiques shallow understanding and underlines the philosopher's role in leading society with wisdom, emphasizing the need for enlightened leadership.

## MEDIEVAL PHILOSOPHY

### 1. The Vision of Hildegard of Bingen

**Timeline:** Hildegard of Bingen (1098–1179 CE)

**Anecdote:** Hildegard of Bingen, a medieval abbess and mystic, claimed to receive divine visions, which influenced her writings on theology, medicine and music. She was a religious reformer who used her influence to challenge and advocate reform within the Church.

**Sociopolitical Significance:** In a society dominated by men, Hildegard's intellectual contributions showed that women could be powerful thinkers and leaders. Her works bridged religion and reason, influencing both religious and intellectual movements of the time.

## MODERN PHILOSOPHY

### 1. Nietzsche and the Death of God

**Timeline:** Friedrich Nietzsche (1844–1900 CE); publication of *The Gay Science* (1882 CE).

**Anecdote:** Nietzsche shocked the world by declaring, 'God is dead,' in *The Gay Science*. He used this statement to describe how traditional religious beliefs were losing their hold on society.

Why the title *The Gay Science*? It refers to the Provençal tradition of 'gai saber' (meaning 'joyful knowledge'), a term used by medieval troubadours or poets to describe the art of song and poetry. Nietzsche chose it to symbolize a free, unburdened and creative search for knowledge, beyond dogmas and traditional constraints. For Nietzsche, 'gay' reflects a sense of lightness, affirmation and celebration of existence.

**Sociopolitical Significance:** Nietzsche's statement captured the cultural shifts of nineteenth-century Europe, marked by the rise of science, industrialization and secularism. His philosophy challenged long-held beliefs, calling for the re-evaluation of ethics and values in a world where human actions and technology were reshaping reality.

# 3

# DEFINING MOMENTS IN PHILOSOPHY

## *Ideas that Changed the World*

### ANCIENT PHILOSOPHY

#### 1. The Trial and Death of Socrates (399 BCE)

**Significance:** Socrates' trial and subsequent execution by hemlock for his philosophical teachings and alleged corruption of Athenian youth became a defining moment in Western philosophy. This event exemplified the tension between innovative philosophical thought and traditional societal norms. His martyrdom highlighted the importance of intellectual integrity and the courage to stand by one's beliefs, even in the face of severe opposition. Socrates' death set the stage for the importance of ethics, reason and critical thinking in Western thought.

#### 2. The Birth of Formal Logic (Fourth Century BCE)

**Significance:** Aristotle's work on formal logic in his *Organon* set the foundation for structured reasoning and became a groundbreaking moment in Western philosophy. His syllogistic reasoning systemized argumentation, deeply influencing law, science and philosophy. Formal logic became the bedrock of systematic inquiry, shaping the way humans understand and reason about the world.

### 3. The Foundation of the Library of Alexandria (Third Century BCE, Ptolemaic Era)

**Significance:** Established under the reign of Ptolemy II Philadelphus, the Library of Alexandria became a centre of knowledge in the Hellenistic era. As one of the first major research institutions, it attracted scholars from across the known world, promoting advancements in a variety of fields, including mathematics, astronomy, philosophy and medicine. It preserved Greek texts and helped ensure intellectual progress, bridging cultures and intellectual traditions for centuries to come.

## MEDIEVAL PHILOSOPHY

### 4. The Translation Movement in Islamic Spain (Eighth–Thirteenth Centuries, Umayyads (661–750 CE) and Abbasids (750–1258 CE)

**Historical Context:** During the Islamic Golden Age, scholars translated Greek and Roman texts into Arabic in cities like Toledo and Baghdad. These works were later reintroduced in Europe through Latin translations, sparking Scholasticism and the preservation of critical knowledge.

**Significance:** This intellectual exchange facilitated the transmission of classical philosophy, science and mathematics to medieval Europe, laying the foundation for the European Renaissance. It demonstrated the transformative power of cross-cultural collaboration in shaping intellectual progress.

### 5. The Synthesis of Aristotelian Philosophy and Christian Theology by St. Thomas Aquinas (1225–74 CE, Scholasticism)

**Significance:** Aquinas' *Summa Theologica* harmonized reason and faith. This synthesis deeply influenced both Christian thought and the Renaissance, providing a framework to discuss metaphysical issues within a religious context, reconciling philosophy with religious belief.

## MODERN PHILOSOPHY

### 6. The Trial of Galileo (1633 CE, Under Pope Urban VIII's Regime)

**Historical Context:** Galileo Galilei's trial by the Roman Inquisition occurred for advocating the heliocentric model of the solar system, contradicting the Church's geocentric doctrine. Galileo's defence of empirical evidence challenged the Church's authority

**Significance:** The trial reflected the Church's resistance to scientific progress and its attempts to maintain authority amidst the Protestant Reformation and Counter-Reformation. Galileo's persecution became emblematic of the tension between reason and dogma, inspiring the Enlightenment's commitment to empirical knowledge and intellectual freedom.

### 7. The Publication of *The Communist Manifesto* (1848 CE)

**Significance:** Written by Karl Marx and Friedrich Engels, *The Communist Manifesto* critiqued the exploitation inherent in capitalist societies and proposed a revolutionary framework for societal change. Its ideas had a profound influence on political philosophy, inspiring global movements for justice, equality and systemic reform.

### 8. The Development of Existentialism (Twentieth Century)

**Significance:** Existentialism, spearheaded by thinkers like Jean-Paul Sartre, Simone de Beauvoir and Martin Heidegger, explored themes of individual freedom, responsibility and authenticity in a world without inherent meaning. Emerging in the aftermath of World War II, it helped grapple with the questions of human existence, moral ambiguities and existential crises of modernity.

## From Thought to Governance: The Rise of Political Philosophy

In this journey, from ancient to modern philosophy, we have explored how philosophical inquiry has responded to and shaped the evolving sociopolitical, cultural and religious landscapes of human civilization. Philosophy has served as both a mirror reflecting the times and a catalyst for shaping them. Next, we will shift our focus to political philosophy as a distinct branch of thought, examining how thinkers began to address questions of governance, justice and power. We will explore how political philosophy emerged from individual ethics to collective concerns and how its development laid the foundation for the systems and structures that define modern societies.

This exploration will uncover how political philosophy has continuously grappled with issues of authority, liberty and community throughout history.

# 4

# THE EVOLUTION OF POLITICAL PHILOSOPHY

## *From Ancient Foundations to Renaissance Reforms*

### Understanding Political Philosophy

Political philosophy is the systematic exploration of fundamental questions about governance, justice, power, rights and the nature of the state. It seeks to answer questions like: What is justice? What is the best form of government? How should power and resources be distributed within a society? Unlike political science, which focuses on empirical analysis, political philosophy deals with normative and ethical questions, shaping the foundations of political systems and ideologies.

This chapter traces the historical evolution of political philosophy, exploring its origins in ancient Greece, its transformation during the Hellenistic and medieval periods and its revival during the Renaissance.

## 1. Ancient Origins: The Classical Foundations of Political Philosophy

The roots of political philosophy can be traced back to ancient Greece, where the polis, or city-state, served as the focal point for political organization and thought. Greek philosophers questioned the nature of justice, citizenship and governance, laying the foundation for Western political thought.

- **Socrates** (c. 470–399 BCE) – The Father of Ethical Inquiry:

  Socrates, known for his Socratic method, a style of dialectical questioning aimed at uncovering universal truths, believed governance should be guided by moral integrity rather than public opinion. Unlike the Sophists, who taught rhetoric for personal gain, Socrates argued that the pursuit of ethical knowledge was the key to a good life. His trial and execution for allegedly corrupting the youth of Athens highlights the tension between philosophical inquiry and societal norms.
- **Plato** (c. 428/427–348/347 BCE) – The Vision of an Ideal State:

  In *The Republic*, Plato envisioned an ideal society governed by 'philosopher-kings' – individuals who possess both wisdom and virtue. He argued that justice arises when each individual fulfils their natural role within a structured hierarchy. His 'allegory of the cave', which contrasts the enlightened philosopher with the ignorant masses, underscores his belief that true knowledge is essential for just governance.

Plato's ideas influenced centuries of political thought, emphasizing the importance of education and moral leadership.

- **Aristotle** (384–322 BCE) – Political Realism and the Common Good:

  Aristotle, Plato's student, diverged from his teacher by focusing on practical governance rather than ideal states. In *Politics*, he categorized governments into monarchies, aristocracies and democracies, evaluating each based on their potential to achieve the common good. Aristotle introduced the concept of the 'polity', a mixed government that balances elements of democracy and oligarchy. His emphasis on constitutional governance and civic virtue has profoundly influenced modern democratic systems.
- **Roman Contributions** – Cicero and the Rule of Law:

  The Roman Republic adapted Greek philosophical principles, emphasizing the importance of law and citizenship. Cicero (106–43 BCE), a statesman and philosopher, argued for natural law – universal moral principles that transcend human legislation. His works, such as *De Republica* and *De Legibus*, emphasized justice as the foundation of political stability and the role of the state in protecting individual rights. Cicero's ideas bridged Greek philosophy and the Roman legal tradition, influencing the development of Western political thought.

**2. The Hellenistic Period: Personal Ethics and Universalism**

Following the conquests of Alexander the Great, the Hellenistic period (323–31 BCE) saw a shift in political thought.

As Greek city-states gave way to empires, philosophers turned their focus from civic engagement to personal ethics and universal principles.

- **Stoicism and the Universal State:**
  Zeno of Citium (c. 334–262 BCE) founded Stoicism, which highlighted living in harmony with nature and adhering to reason. Stoics like Marcus Aurelius expanded this philosophy, advocating for rulers to embody virtue and align their actions with natural law. The Stoic idea of a universal state, where all humans are citizens of a single moral community, influenced early Christian political thought and later concepts of human rights.
- **Epicureanism** – A Retreat from Politics:
  Epicurus (341–270 BCE) viewed politics with scepticism, seeing it as a source of unnecessary conflict. He advocated for withdrawal from public life to seek happiness through friendship and philosophical contemplation. While less politically engaged than Stoicism, Epicureanism offered an alternative perspective on the role of governance, stressing personal autonomy over collective authority.

### 3. Medieval Political Thought: The Synthesis of Faith and Reason

The fall of the Roman Empire and the rise of Christianity transformed political philosophy. Medieval thinkers sought to reconcile Greek and Roman ideas with Christian theology, emphasizing the divine origins of political authority.

- **Augustine of Hippo** (354–430 CE) – *The City of God*:
  In *The City of God*, Augustine distinguished between the 'City of Man', driven by earthly desires, and the 'City of God', a divine order of peace and justice. He argued that earthly governance was necessary to restrain sin and maintain order, but it must ultimately align with God's will. Augustine's work shaped medieval political thought by emphasizing the moral responsibilities of rulers.
- **Thomas Aquinas** (1225–74 CE) – Natural Law and Legitimate Authority:
  Aquinas' *Summa Theologica* synthesized Aristotelian philosophy with Christian theology, arguing that natural law, a moral order discernible through reason, was the basis of legitimate political authority. Aquinas stressed that rulers must serve the common good and uphold justice, laying the groundwork for modern constitutional theory. His ideas on the relationship between church and state influenced debates on governance for centuries.
- **Islamic Contributions** – Al-Farabi and Ibn Khaldun:
  Islamic philosophers preserved and expanded Greek political philosophy during the medieval period. Al-Farabi (872–950 CE) described an ideal society in *The Virtuous City*, blending Platonic ideals with Islamic ethics. Ibn Khaldun (1332–1406 CE), in his *Muqaddimah*, introduced concepts of social cohesion, historical cycles and the dynamics of power, which prefigured modern sociology and political science.

## 4. The Renaissance: Humanism and Secular Governance

The Renaissance (fourteenth–seventeenth centuries) marked a rebirth of classical learning, with political philosophy reflecting the humanistic emphasis on individual potential and secular governance.

- **Niccolò Machiavelli** (1469–1527 CE) – Pragmatism over Idealism:

  In *The Prince*, Machiavelli broke with medieval traditions by separating ethics from politics. He argued that rulers must prioritize power and stability over morality, advocating for 'realpolitik' . While often criticized for its cynicism, Machiavelli's work laid the foundation for modern political science by underscoring the realities of governance rather than idealized theories.
- **Erasmus** (1466–1536 CE) – The Moral Critique:

  Erasmus, a leading humanist, critiqued corruption within the church and state in works like *The Praise of Folly*. He stressed ethical leadership and the need for rulers to prioritize justice and compassion. Erasmus' humanistic approach reflected the broader Renaissance effort to reform political and religious institutions.
- **The Printing Revolution and Political Thought:**

  The invention of the printing press by Johannes Gutenberg (c. 1440 CE) revolutionized the dissemination of political ideas. Texts like *The Prince* and *The Praise of Folly* reached wider audiences, fostering debate and challenging traditional authority. The printing press played a pivotal role in the spread of Renaissance humanism and the Reformation.

- **Foundations for Modern Political Philosophy:** By the end of the Renaissance, political philosophy had evolved from its ancient focus on ethical governance to embrace pragmatic approaches, individual rights and the interplay between morality and power. These developments laid the groundwork for the Enlightenment's emphasis on reason, liberty and social contract theory, which would further transform political thought.

## THE EVOLUTION OF POLITICAL PHILOSOPHY: ENLIGHTENMENT TO MODERN TIMES

Building on the foundational principles established from ancient times through the Renaissance, the evolution of political philosophy during the Enlightenment and modern periods reflects humanity's growing emphasis on reason, individual liberty and critiques of power structures. The Enlightenment introduced transformative ideas about rights, democracy and governance, while modern philosophy grappled with challenges posed by capitalism, industrialization, identity politics and global conflicts.

### 5. The Enlightenment: The Age of Reason and Rights

The Enlightenment (seventeenth–eighteenth centuries) was a period of intellectual awakening that prioritized reason, science and scepticism of authority. Political philosophy underwent a seismic shift, advocating for individual rights and reshaping governance structures.

- **Thomas Hobbes** (1588–1679 CE) – The Social Contract and Sovereignty:

  In *Leviathan*, Hobbes developed a framework for the social contract, arguing that individuals in the state of nature lived in a chaotic and violent condition. To escape this, they formed a contract, ceding their rights to a sovereign authority in exchange for security and order. Although criticized for its authoritarian tone, Hobbes's work profoundly influenced later political theorists and introduced foundational concepts of state legitimacy and authority.
- **John Locke** (1632–1704 CE) – The Father of Liberalism:

  Locke's *Two Treatises of Government* laid the groundwork for liberal democracy. Rejecting absolute monarchy, Locke argued that governments derive their legitimacy from the consent of the governed. His assertion that individuals have natural rights to life, liberty and property inspired revolutions and the development of constitutional democracies.
- **Jean-Jacques Rousseau** (1712–78 CE) – The General Will:

  Rousseau's *The Social Contract* emphasized the concept of the 'general will', suggesting that true political authority comes from the collective will of the people. While his advocacy for participatory democracy inspired revolutionary movements, Rousseau's ideas also raised concerns about balancing individual freedoms with collective interests.
- **Montesquieu** (1689–1755 CE) – Separation of Powers.

  Montesquieu's *The Spirit of the Laws* articulated the principle of separating governmental powers into executive, legislative and judicial branches. This idea became a cornerstone of modern constitutional governance, influencing the structures of democracies worldwide.

## 6. Modern Political Philosophy: Confronting New Realities

The modern era (nineteenth–twenty-first centuries) saw political philosophy responding to challenges posed by industrialization, capitalism and global conflicts. Thinkers addressed themes of inequality, freedom and power, often critiquing existing systems.

- **Karl Marx** (1818–83) – The Critique of Capitalism: Marx's *The Communist Manifesto* and *Das Kapital* critiqued the capitalist system, arguing that economic structures determine political and social relationships. He advocated for the overthrow of capitalist systems to establish a classless, stateless society. Marx's theories have deeply influenced political ideologies and movements worldwide.
- **John Stuart Mill** (1806–73) – Liberty and Utilitarianism: Mill's *On Liberty* emphasized the importance of individual freedom, introducing the 'harm principle', which argues that state intervention is justified only to prevent harm to others. His *Utilitarianism* proposed that moral and political decisions should aim for the greatest happiness for the greatest number. Mill's progressive views on free speech and gender equality remain influential.

- **Friedrich Nietzsche** (1844–1900) – Power and Morality:

  Nietzsche challenged the foundations of Western morality, famously declaring, 'God is dead.' In *Thus Spoke Zarathustra*, he critiqued the values underpinning political systems and advocated for the creation of new values through individual will. Nietzsche's ideas influenced existentialist and postmodernist political philosophies.
- **Max Weber** (1864–1920) – Bureaucracy and Legitimacy:

  Weber's *Economy and Society* explored the rationalization of authority in modern states. He introduced the concept of 'legitimacy', classifying authority into traditional, charismatic and rational-legal types. His analysis of bureaucracy as an efficient but potentially dehumanizing structure remains relevant in understanding modern governance.

## 7. Twentieth-Century Political Philosophy: Identity, Justice and Rights

The twentieth-century brought new challenges, including world wars, decolonization and civil rights movements. Political philosophy evolved to address issues of identity, justice and systemic oppression.

- **Hannah Arendt** (1906–75) – Totalitarianism and Public Space:

  In *The Origins of Totalitarianism*, Arendt analysed the rise of totalitarian regimes, exploring how mass societies erode individuality. She stressed the importance of public spaces for political deliberation and action, advocating for active participation as a cornerstone of democracy.

- **John Rawls** (1921–2002) – Justice as Fairness:
  Rawls' *A Theory of Justice* introduced 'justice as fairness', proposing principles of justice derived from a hypothetical 'original position' behind a 'veil of ignorance'. His egalitarian approach reshaped discussions on distributive justice and influenced welfare policies globally.
- **Frantz Fanon** (1925–1961) – Decolonization and Identity:
  In *The Wretched of the Earth*, Fanon examined the psychological and political impacts of colonization, advocating for revolutionary struggle to reclaim autonomy. His work remains foundational in postcolonial political thought.

**8. Gender and Queer Theories: Reshaping Political Philosophy**

Contemporary political philosophy has increasingly recognized the role of gender and queer theories in challenging traditional structures of power and governance.

- **Judith Butler** (1956–present) – Gender Performativity:
  In *Gender Trouble*, Butler introduced the concept of gender performativity, arguing that gender is not innate but constructed through repeated actions. This critique of essentialism has profound implications for how political systems recognize and address identity.
- **Bell Hooks** (1952–2021) – Intersectionality and Marginalized Voices:
  Hooks's work emphasized the interplay of race, gender and class in shaping oppression. Her critiques of patriarchy and capitalism have pushed political philosophy to adopt more inclusive frameworks.

- **Queer Theories** – Reimagining Political Agency:
  Queer theorists like Eve Kosofsky Sedgwick and José Esteban Muñoz challenged heteronormative assumptions, advocating for political systems that embrace fluid and diverse identities. Their work has broadened the scope of citizenship and agency in political thought.

## CONCLUSION: THE DYNAMIC EVOLUTION OF POLITICAL PHILOSOPHY

The evolution of political philosophy reflects humanity's enduring struggle to balance power, justice and liberty. From the Enlightenment's focus on reason and individual rights to modern critiques of capitalism and identity politics, political philosophy remains a vital lens for analysing and reshaping society. By grappling with the complexities of governance, freedom and identity, it continues to inspire movements for a more just and equitable world.

### Looking Ahead: Bridging the Past and Present

Over time, political philosophy has moved beyond broad theoretical frameworks to engage deeply with real-world issues of governance, justice, identity and resistance. The core ideas explored in this chapter – Plato's vision of justice, Hobbes' social contract, Marx's critique of capitalism or Butler's gender performativity – have not only shaped political structures but also influenced the way these ideas are taught, debated and reinterpreted across generations.

In the next chapter, we delve into the intellectual journeys of key philosophers, examining their pedagogical methods, their engagement with political structures and their lasting impact on the study of political thought. From the Socratic method's emphasis on dialectical questioning to Rousseau's vision of participatory democracy and Arendt's exploration of authority and totalitarianism, each thinker has contributed uniquely to the pedagogical tradition of political philosophy.

By tracing these individual contributions, we will uncover how the teaching and dissemination of political philosophy has sparked intellectual movements, influenced policy debates and continue to inspire critical thought in contemporary academia.

# 5

# THE THINKERS WHO SHAPED POLITICAL PHILOSOPHY

Political philosophy isn't just about abstract theories – it's a story of bold ideas, intense debates, and the search for a just society. This chapter will take you on a journey through the lives and legacies of some of history's most influential thinkers, each wrestling with fundamental questions: What makes a society fair? How should power be distributed? What rights do individuals have against the state?

From Socrates, who challenged people to question everything, to Rawls, whose vision of justice still shapes modern policies, these philosophers responded to the struggles of their time – wars, revolutions and shifting ideologies – by offering ideas that continue to resonate today. Their theories weren't just academic exercises; they were blueprints for real-world change.

This chapter isn't just about their contributions but seeks to make their ideas accessible, breaking down complex concepts into conversations that feel relevant to our everyday lives. Because, at its core, political philosophy isn't just a subject to study; it is a way to understand the world, the power structures that shape it and our role within them.

## SOCRATES: THE FATHER OF PHILOSOPHY

### Historical Context and Introduction

Socrates, born in Athens around 470 BCE, lived in a time of political instability and changing values. He is considered one of the most influential figures in Western philosophy. As Athens struggled with the aftermath of war and the challenges of early democracy, Socrates questioned the status quo, becoming a voice for critical thinking and moral introspection.

Instead of cosmological theories, his work focused on human ethics shaping political philosophy around justice, virtue and the role of citizens in a state.

### Brief Biography

Born to Sophroniscus, a stonemason, and Phaenarete, a midwife, Socrates likely assisted his father in masonry as a youth. This upbringing instilled in him a practical approach to life and an appreciation for craftsmanship, which later influenced his belief that moral excellence requires continuous effort and refinement, much like a skilled craft.

Socrates served as a hoplite (infantryman) in the Peloponnesian War (431–404 BCE), participating in critical battles, like the Battle of Potidaea (432 BCE), where he reportedly saved the life of Alcibiades (450–404 BCE), a prominent Athenian statesman and general, during this conflict; the Battle of Delium (424 BCE), where he was noted for his endurance and calm retreat after the Athenian defeat, showcasing his philosophical principles in action; the Battle of Amphipolis (422 BCE), which marked another critical moment of his civic duty and physical resilience.

Socrates' military service embodied his belief in courage (Andreia) as a key virtue and reinforced his disdain for self-indulgence, which he saw as antithetical to the disciplined life required for moral excellence.

Socrates himself wrote nothing; what we know of him comes from his disciples, primarily Plato and Xenophon. He was, however, influenced by philosophers like Anaxagoras (500–428 BCE), who introduced him to the concept of nous (mind), Heraclitus (535–475 BCE), whose doctrine of change, influenced Socrates' view of the dynamic nature of virtue and knowledge and the Sophists (fifth century BCE), whose focus on rhetoric and human-centred inquiry pushed him to explore objective standards of truth and virtue.

Known for his humble demeanor, Socrates, by his early thirties, had abandoned the life of a stonemason to pursue philosophy full-time. He spent his days in Athens at the agora (marketplace), questioning anyone willing to engage in conversation, pushing them to examine their lives and beliefs.

His open-air debates became his signature, the Socratic Method, a form of dialogue aimed at uncovering assumptions and arriving at truth through questioning.

His pursuit of truth led to his trial and death sentence for 'corrupting the youth' and impiety. He chose death over abandoning his philosophy.

## Core Contribution to Political Philosophy

Socrates revolutionized philosophy by focusing on practical questions about life instead of metaphysical speculation.

Instead of giving answers, he asked questions, making philosophy a tool for critical thinking and self-awareness. Let us look at some of his contributions and their significance:

**The Socratic Method:** Socrates pioneered a dialogical method aimed at exposing contradictions in beliefs and deepening understanding.

*Example:* In Plato's *Apology*, Socrates questions his accusers, revealing their lack of clarity about justice and piety.

*Significance*: This method laid the foundation for modern critical thinking, pedagogy and the dialectical approach in philosophy.

**Focus on Ethics and Virtue:** Socrates shifted the focus of philosophy from natural sciences to human morality, arguing that a virtuous life is the highest goal and true knowledge is tied to moral action (virtue is knowledge).

*Example*: In *Meno*, Socrates argues that virtue can be taught and equates it with knowledge, emphasizing that ignorance leads to wrongdoing.

*Significance*: His philosophy influenced ethical theories, shaping later thinkers like Aristotle's virtue ethics and Kant's moral philosophy.

**Rejection of Relativism:** Socrates believed in universal truths about virtue and justice, opposing the Sophists' view that 'man is the measure of all things'.

*Example*: In Gorgias, Socrates debates the sophist Callicles, arguing that might does not make right and that justice is not merely a social construct.

*Significance*: This stance became central to Western philosophy, inspiring later thinkers like Plato (427–347 BCE) and Immanuel Kant (1724–1804 CE).

**Challenging Traditional Beliefs, Critique of Athenian Democracy:** Socrates questioned the legitimacy of Athenian democracy, particularly its emphasis on majority rule over informed decision-making. He believed governance should be led by those with moral and intellectual wisdom, akin to the captain of a ship.

*Example*: In Plato's *Republic*, Socrates suggests that philosopher–kings would govern more justly than elected officials swayed by popular opinion.

*Significance*: His critique exposed the fragility of democratic systems and raised enduring questions about the role of expertise in governance.

**Criticism of Religion and Traditional Morality:** Socrates challenged traditional Greek beliefs about gods, arguing for a moral framework based on reason rather than mythology. His questioning of divine authority contributed to the accusations during his trial for impiety.

*Example*: In *Euthyphro*, Socrates asks, 'Is something pious because the gods love it, or do the gods love it because it is pious?' This exposed contradictions in religious beliefs.

*Significance*: This approach influenced theological and philosophical discussions for centuries, bridging morality with rational inquiry.

**Critique of the Sophists' Relativism:** Socrates opposed the sophists' relativism and commercialized teaching of rhetoric, arguing that their focus on persuasion undermined the pursuit of truth.

*Example*: Socrates believed that the sophists' methods prioritized winning arguments over seeking knowledge, which he saw as detrimental to ethical development.

*Significance*: His emphasis on truth-seeking over rhetorical skill set a precedent for philosophical rigour.

**Philosophy Over Wealth and Power:** Socrates rejected materialism and the pursuit of wealth, advocating instead for a life devoted to self-examination and ethical growth.

*Example*: He famously said, 'The unexamined life is not worth living.'

*Significance*: This revolutionary idea reshaped philosophy, highlighting introspection and moral development over external success.

His constant questioning of assumptions about ethics, politics and society inspired future philosophers to explore the nature of justice, democracy and the role of the individual within the state.

**The Trial and Execution of Socrates**

**The Charges Against Socrates:** In 399 BCE, Socrates was brought to trial on charges of:

1. Impiety (asebeia): Accused of failing to recognize the gods of Athens and introducing new deities.

2. Corrupting the youth of Athens: Allegedly leading young Athenians away from traditional values through his questioning and critiques.

These charges were likely motivated by broader political and social tensions rather than any specific actions by Socrates. Athens, reeling from its defeat in the Peloponnesian War (431–404 BCE) and the tyranny of the Thirty Tyrants (404 BCE), was deeply divided.

Socrates' association with controversial figures like Critias, a leader of the Thirty Tyrants, further fuelled suspicion.

**The *Apology* and Socrates' Defense:** Socrates' trial is immortalized in Plato's *Apology*, where he presents a spirited defence of his philosophy and life. Let us look at the key arguments in his defence:

1. Socrates claimed to be fulfilling a divine mission to question and challenge assumptions, likening himself to a 'gadfly' stinging the 'noble but sluggish horse' of Athens.
2. He argued that he never intentionally corrupted the youth and invited his accusers to provide evidence, which they failed to do.
3. Socrates maintained that his quest for truth was not impiety but a deeper form of reverence for the divine.

Despite his eloquence, Socrates was found guilty by a narrow margin and sentenced to death.

**Execution by Hemlock:** Socrates was offered the chance to go into exile, but he refused, arguing that it would undermine his principles and respect for the rule of law.

In Plato's *Crito*, Socrates reasons that accepting the penalty is a moral obligation to the city-state, even if the law was unjustly applied.

In Plato's *Phaedo*, Socrates faces his execution with remarkable calm, discussing the immortality of the soul with his followers before drinking the cup of hemlock.

**Impact of Socrates' Death:** Socrates' execution marked a pivotal moment in Western philosophy, transforming him into a martyr for truth and intellectual freedom. His death became a critique of Athens' democratic system, highlighting its vulnerability to mob rule and political scapegoating.

**Legacy:** Socrates' trial and execution inspired his students, particularly Plato (427–347 BCE), to preserve and expand his teachings, ensuring his ideas would influence generations.

## ANECDOTES

### 1. Socrates and Alcibiades

Socrates mentored Alcibiades (450–404 BCE), a charismatic but morally conflicted Athenian general. Despite Socrates' efforts to instil virtue, Alcibiades pursued personal ambition and betrayed Athens.

This illustrates Socrates' belief that moral guidance is crucial but ultimately depends on the individual's choices.

### 2. The Day of Execution

In Plato's *Phaedo*, Socrates calmly discusses the immortality of the soul with his disciples before drinking the hemlock.

Socrates' composure and philosophical reflections in his final moments demonstrate his commitment to reason and virtue, even in the face of death.

### 3. Philosophizing in the Agora

Socrates spent his days in the Athenian agora (marketplace), engaging citizens in debates about ethics and governance, often making enemies among the powerful. His public questioning challenged societal norms, laying the groundwork for critical thinking and participatory discourse.

### Why His Ideas Matter Today

Socrates' legacy lives on in modern democratic debates and discussions. He challenged traditional power and promoted free speech, shaping civil discourse in contemporary politics. His method of inquiry is still key in education, especially in law and political science. The idea that questioning our values leads to a just society continues to guide governance and ethical responsibility even today.

## PLATO: THE VISIONARY OF IDEALISM

### Historical Context and Introduction

Plato, a student of Socrates and a teacher to Aristotle, was born in Athens around 428 BCE. Known as the Classical Period, this era saw monumental achievements in art, drama and architecture. Athens was home to the Parthenon, the tragedies of Sophocles and the birth of democracy. Yet, beneath this flourishing exterior lay profound challenges.

It was a time of political upheaval after Athens lost the Peloponnesian War against Sparta, signalling the collapse of its empire. Democratic ideals, once a source of pride, were increasingly undermined by corruption and factionalism. The brief but brutal rule of the Thirty Tyrants, a pro-Spartan oligarchy, exacerbated tensions, leaving Athens in moral and political disarray.

For young Plato, these contradictions were formative. Athens was a paradox: a city renowned for its intellectual vibrancy yet plagued by moral decline and political unrest. This duality profoundly shaped his critique of democracy and inspired his vision of an ideal state governed by reason and justice.

Athens also served as a fertile ground for intellectual growth. Philosophers like Heraclitus and Pythagoras had laid the groundwork for metaphysical inquiry, while sophists challenged traditional notions of truth and virtue. Most importantly, Athens was home to Socrates, whose teachings would become the cornerstone of Plato's philosophy.

Plato absorbed this rich intellectual heritage, synthesizing it into a cohesive vision that sought to address the challenges of his time. Concerned with the flaws in society and governance, he sought answers to questions of justice, governance and the ideal state, giving birth to ideas that continue to shape political theory and philosophy.

### Brief Biography

Plato was born Aristocles to an aristocratic family. His father, Ariston, claimed descent from the early kings of Athens while his mother, Perictione, was related to Solon, the famed Athenian lawgiver. This prestigious lineage afforded Plato access to the finest education available, encompassing poetry, music, gymnastics and philosophy.

Plato came from a wealthy and influential family, but he rejected a life of politics to follow philosophy. His encounter with Socrates transformed his life. Under Socrates' mentorship, Plato abandoned his literary ambitions and turned to philosophy, captivated by the quest for wisdom and the examination of ethical questions.

Socrates was not just a teacher to Plato; he was a profound moral and intellectual influence. Socrates' dialectic method of questioning became the foundation of Plato's own philosophical style, appearing throughout his dialogues as a tool to probe complex ideas.

After witnessing the trial and death of Socrates in 399 BCE, he was deeply affected. For him, the trial epitomized the failure of democratic governance to uphold wisdom and virtue. Witnessing Socrates' unjust death strengthened Plato's resolve to imagine a society where reason and justice, rather than popular opinion, would guide decisions.

Plato preserved Socrates' legacy in *Dialogues*, which depict Socrates engaging in conversations about truth, morality and the nature of the soul. Though he wrote extensively, it is in *Dialogues* that we find his most famous philosophical ideas. It ensured that Socrates' teachings continued to influence generations of thinkers, cementing his role as a foundational figure in Western philosophy.

Plato also embarked on a series of travels that expanded his intellectual horizons and deepened his philosophical insights. His journeys took him to Egypt, where he studied geometry, astronomy and religious practices. Egyptian mathematics, with its focus on precision and abstraction, influenced Plato's approach to metaphysical questions. Similarly, Egyptian religious traditions, which emphasized the immortality of the soul, resonated with Plato's developing ideas about the Theory of Forms.

In southern Italy, Plato encountered the Pythagoreans, a philosophical community that emphasized the importance of mathematical harmony and cosmic order. The Pythagoreans believed that numbers were the ultimate reality, an idea that aligned with Plato's Theory of Forms. Their influence is evident in Plato's use of mathematical principles to explore metaphysical and ethical questions.

Plato's travels were not merely academic; they were a quest for universal truths. He sought to integrate diverse traditions into a coherent system of thought, blending Greek rationalism with insights from other cultures. This cosmopolitan perspective is reflected in his works, which address both individual and societal concerns.

Upon returning to Athens around 387 BCE, Plato founded the Academy, an institution of higher learning dedicated to the pursuit of knowledge and the cultivation of wisdom. The Academy became a hub of intellectual activity, attracting students like Aristotle and fostering debates on topics ranging from ethics to astronomy. Plato's experiences abroad enriched his vision for the Academy, which combined rigourous inquiry with a commitment to moral and intellectual development.

### Core Contribution to Political Philosophy

Plato's most significant contribution to political philosophy is his concept of the 'ideal state', as outlined in *The Republic*. It is a cornerstone of Western philosophy and political theory. In this dialogue, Plato explores the fundamental nature of justice and presents his vision of an ideal state, governed by philosopher-kings, the leaders equipped with wisdom and knowledge of the eternal forms. These rulers prioritize the common good over personal ambition, embodying Plato's belief in the necessity of rational and virtuous governance. Central to *The Republic* is Plato's division of society into three classes:

1. Philosopher-kings: Rulers guided by reason and wisdom, responsible for making decisions in the best interest of society.
2. Auxiliaries: The warrior class, tasked with enforcing laws and defending the state.
3. Producers: Farmers, artisans and merchants who sustain the economy through their labour and skills.

Plato posits that justice emerges when each class performs its designated role without overstepping its boundaries. For example, producers should not attempt to govern, and rulers should not be swayed by material desires. Justice, in Plato's view, is a harmonious alignment of individual and societal virtues, achieved through specialization and adherence to one's natural role.

Plato's critique of democracy is a recurring theme in *The Republic*. He argues that democratic systems prioritize popularity over competence, often elevating unqualified individuals to positions of power. This can lead to chaos, inefficiency and the erosion of justice. Plato's ideal state, by contrast, is hierarchical, with philosopher-kings at the helm, ensuring decisions are guided by reason and virtue rather than fleeting public opinion. Plato's concept of justice has greatly influenced subsequent political thought, inspiring debates on the balance between liberty and order, as well as the role of expertise in governance. His vision continues to challenge modern democracies to reconcile individual freedoms with the need for collective harmony.

Plato was sceptical of democracy. Having seen Athens fail, especially in the trial of Socrates, he criticized a system where decisions relied on popular opinion rather than wisdom.

### The Allegory of the Cave

One of the most compelling sections of *The Republic* is the allegory of the cave, a vivid metaphor for the human condition and the transformative power of education. Plato describes prisoners chained in a dark cave, their gaze fixed on a wall where shadows of objects cast by a fire appear. For the prisoners, these shadows constitute reality. When one prisoner escapes and ventures into the outside world, he discovers the true nature of reality – bright, vivid and far richer than the shadows he once knew.

This allegory represents the philosopher's journey from ignorance to enlightenment. The cave symbolizes the limited perspective of those who rely solely on sensory experiences, while the outside world represents the realm of the forms – unchanging, eternal truths accessible through intellectual reasoning. The sun, in this metaphor, represents the Form of the Good, the ultimate source of knowledge and reality.

The allegory also serves as an analysis of humanity's tendency to accept appearances at face value. In modern times, it resonates with issues like media manipulation, misinformation and the challenges of breaking free from societal or ideological constraints. It encourages readers to question the shadows they see and seek deeper truths beyond superficial realities.

Interestingly, the allegory of the cave bears a striking resemblance to concepts in Indian philosophy, particularly the notion of maya in Vedanta. Like Plato's shadows, maya represents the illusion of the material world, which veils the true nature of ultimate reality. Both traditions emphasize the role of intellectual and spiritual awakening in transcending this illusion. This parallel highlights the universality of Plato's insights and their resonance with diverse philosophical traditions.

## Plato's Educational Philosophy

For Plato, education was not merely about imparting knowledge but about shaping character and cultivating the virtues necessary for individual and societal excellence. He envisioned education as a lifelong process aimed at harmonizing the soul's three parts:

1. Rational: Developing wisdom and critical thinking
2. Spirited: Instilling courage and resilience
3. Appetitive: Cultivating temperance and self-control

Plato's Academy, founded around 387 BCE, embodied this holistic approach. As the first institution of higher learning in the Western world, the Academy stressed on interdisciplinary study, blending mathematics, astronomy, philosophy and ethics. It encouraged students to engage in dialogue and critical inquiry, fostering intellectual independence and moral growth.

The Academy's impact on future academic systems cannot be overstated. It inspired the development of universities in medieval Europe and laid the foundation for the liberal arts tradition. Plato's emphasis on nurturing the soul and intellect continues to influence modern educational philosophies, particularly those that highlight critical thinking and moral development alongside technical knowledge.

## ANECDOTES

### 1. Plato's Duel with the Poets

Plato controversially argued for banning poets from the ideal state because they misled people with illusions rather than truth. However, despite this stance, Plato himself was a brilliant writer, crafting vivid dialogues that often read like dramatic plays.

This paradox highlights Plato's complex relationship with artistic expression – he distrusted its influence yet used it masterfully to communicate philosophy.

### 2. Plato's Influence on Political Exiles

Plato's ideas on governance inspired not just kings but also political exiles and reformers. One notable example is 'Dion of Syracuse', who, after studying under Plato, attempted to overthrow the corrupt rule of Dionysius II and establish a more just government. However, Dion was eventually assassinated.

This episode demonstrates how Plato's political philosophy inspired real-world attempts at reform, often with tragic consequences.

### Why His Ideas Matter Today

Plato's influence extends across disciplines, shaping fields as diverse as philosophy, political theory, education and science.

His Theory of Forms, which posits the existence of eternal, unchanging realities beyond the physical world, has been a cornerstone of metaphysical inquiry. It has inspired debates on the nature of universals, the relationship between the material and the ideal, and the pursuit of truth.

In politics, Plato's concept of philosopher-kings still influences debates on leadership and expertise in governance. While his critique of democracy has often been seen as elitist, it underscores important questions about the qualifications and moral responsibilities of leaders. His ideas challenge modern democracies to balance popular participation with the need for informed decision-making.

Plato's philosophical inquiries continue to resonate in contemporary contexts, addressing issues like media literacy, ethical leadership and the role of education in societal progress. His works remind us that the pursuit of wisdom and justice is an ongoing endeavour, vital for navigating the complexities of the modern world.

## ARISTOTLE: THE PHILOSOPHER OF PRACTICAL WISDOM

### Historical Context and Introduction

Aristotle, a student of Plato and teacher to Alexander the Great, was born in 384 BCE in northern Greece. He lived during the Classical period of Ancient Greece. Aristotle's lifetime coincided with the expansion of Greek thought and its transition from mythological explanations to systematic reasoning.

Unlike Plato, who focused on abstract forms, Aristotle grounded his philosophy in observation and empirical study.

His practical approach made him a key figure in political and philosophical theory.

### Brief Biography

Aristotle's upbringing was steeped in the intellectual traditions of his time. His father, Nicomachus, served as the court physician to King Amyntas III of Macedon. This not only exposed Aristotle to the biological sciences but also to the structured reasoning and empirical methods used in medicine, laying an early foundation for his scientific approach to knowledge.

After his parents passed away, Aristotle was sent to Athens at the age of seventeen to study at Plato's Academy, one of the most prestigious centres of learning in the ancient world. Aristotle immersed himself in the teachings of Plato, engaging with philosophical debates that examined the nature of reality, ethics and governance. He spent twenty years at the Academy before founding his own school, the Lyceum.

Aristotle wrote extensively on subjects like logic, metaphysics, ethics and politics. His works preserved and advanced knowledge for centuries, influencing both Western and Islamic thought.

### Core Contribution to Political Philosophy

Under Plato's mentorship, Aristotle excelled as a student and later as a teacher. Plato's Theory of Forms influenced Aristotle deeply, underlining that true knowledge lies in understanding ideal, unchanging abstractions rather than the mutable physical world.

However, Aristotle eventually diverged from this perspective. He believed that the physical world, accessible through the senses, was central to understanding reality.

Aristotle's unique approach was marked by his empirical methodology. He focused on systematic observation and logical analysis to explain natural phenomena. This divergence from Plato's idealism established Aristotle as an original thinker who emphasized the practical application of philosophy.

## Challenging Traditional Beliefs

Aristotle's rejection of Plato's idealism marked a significant philosophical revolution. While Plato sought truth in transcendent, abstract forms, Aristotle argued that knowledge must be grounded in sensory experience and empirical observation. In works like *Metaphysics*, Aristotle examined the nature of reality, proposing that substances, entities with inherent properties, constitute the essence of existence.

His emphasis on the observable world and systematic categorization transformed natural sciences, ethics and metaphysics. This approach also faced resistance as many scholars clung to established philosophical traditions. Aristotle's commitment to challenging these norms was a defining feature of his intellectual journey.

## The Concept of the Unmoved Mover

The concept of the 'unmoved mover' is central to Aristotle's metaphysical thought. It appears in *Metaphysics*, where Aristotle seeks to explain the fundamental principles of motion, change and existence. He observed that everything in the universe is in motion or subject to change, whether physical, biological or cosmological. For motion to occur, there must be a cause, 'a mover' that initiates the process.

However, Aristotle reasoned that there could not be an infinite regress of movers (a never-ending chain of causes) as this would make motion inexplicable. To resolve this, he proposed the existence of a 'first cause' or 'unmoved mover', that is, an eternal and necessary entity that causes motion without itself being moved or changed.

Aristotle describes this entity as the ultimate source of all motion and change in the universe but not in a direct, mechanical sense. Instead, they inspire motion and order as the ultimate object of desire and purpose. Like a leader whose mere existence motivates followers to act.

In a cosmological sense, the unmoved mover is associated with the heavens and the eternal rotation of celestial spheres. Aristotle saw it as a self-sufficient and divine entity, characterized by pure intellect and contemplation. Its influence lies not in physical interaction but in its perfection, which all beings strive to emulate.

The unmoved mover has been interpreted as a precursor to theological concepts in later traditions, particularly in monotheistic religions. While Aristotle's understanding of divinity differs from modern religious views, his concept remains foundational in discussions of causality, metaphysics and the origins of the universe.

### Emergence of a New Worldview

Aristotle's empirical and systematic approach to understanding reality marked a turning point in Western thought. He created a framework for categorizing and classifying knowledge, which influenced both philosophical and scientific disciplines. His work on logic, outlined in *Organon*, introduced syllogism, a method of deductive reasoning that became a cornerstone of Western intellectual traditions.

In biology, Aristotle's meticulous observations led to the classification of living organisms while his ethical philosophy in *Nicomachean Ethics* emphasized achieving moral virtue through practical wisdom and moderation. These contributions exemplified his commitment to bridging theory with practice.

## Contribution to Art and Creativity

Aristotle's contributions to art and creativity are immortalized in his work *Poetics*, a foundational text in literary theory and criticism. In this treatise, Aristotle examines the principles of storytelling, drama and poetry, offering timeless insights into the nature and purpose of artistic expression. His ideas continue to shape how we understand and create narratives in literature, theatre and film.

He saw art as an imitation (mimesis) of life, emphasizing that storytelling reflects human actions, emotions and experiences. However, this imitation was not mere replication as Plato had suggested. For Aristotle, art transcended reality by presenting a more structured and meaningful version of life, one that inspires reflection and emotional engagement.

In *Poetics*, Aristotle highlights the importance of storytelling as a way to explore universal truths. He famously wrote, 'The aim of art is to represent not the outward appearance of things, but their inward significance.' This belief underscored his view that art plays a critical role in educating, entertaining and morally uplifting society.

Aristotle's *Poetics* also identifies six essential elements that constitute a well-crafted tragedy. These principles continue to guide storytelling across various genres and media:

1. Plot (Mythos): Aristotle considered the plot to be the most important element of a story. He defined it as the arrangement of incidents or events that unfold in a logical sequence – a clear beginning, middle and end – creating a cohesive and unified narrative. He also emphasized the importance of causality, where every event is a consequence of preceding actions.
2. Character (Ethos): While the plot drives the story, the characters bring it to life. Aristotle argued that the protagonist must possess hamartia (a tragic flaw) that leads to their downfall. This flaw makes the character relatable and evokes pity and fear in the audience. For him, the greatest characters were neither wholly good nor wholly evil but morally complex individuals.
3. Thought (Dianoia): It refers to the themes, ideas and messages conveyed through the story. Aristotle valued works that provoked intellectual engagement and moral contemplation. He believed a tragedy should explore profound philosophical or ethical questions.
4. Diction (Lexis): It pertains to the language and style of a work. Aristotle stressed that the choice of words, metaphors and expressions must suit the characters and themes, contributing to the story's overall impact.
5. Song (Melos): Music and rhythm played a significant role in Greek drama. Aristotle highlighted the emotional power of song and how it complements the story's mood and tone. Although music was more central to ancient Greek tragedies, Aristotle's insights remain relevant in the use of soundtracks and rhythm in modern storytelling.
6. Spectacle (Opsis): Spectacle refers to the visual and sensory elements of a performance, such as

costumes, scenery and special effects. While Aristotle acknowledged its importance in engaging the audience, he warned that it should never overshadow the story's substance. 'The spectacle, though an attraction, is the least artistic of all the parts, and has least to do with the art of poetry.

One of Aristotle's most influential ideas in *Poetics* is the concept of catharsis. He argued that tragedy serves a therapeutic purpose by arousing pity and fear in the audience, leading to an emotional purging or cleansing. This cathartic experience allows the audience to confront and release deep-seated emotions, leaving them morally enriched and intellectually stimulated.

His analysis of storytelling laid the foundation for literary theory and continues to influence modern narratives, from classical plays to contemporary cinema. His six elements of storytelling are evident in works ranging from Shakespearean tragedies to Hollywood screenplays, where plot, character and themes remain central to narrative construction.

Through his intense exploration of the human condition and the mechanics of storytelling, Aristotle elevated art to a discipline that not only entertains but also educates and inspires. His insights affirm the enduring power of creativity as a medium for understanding ourselves and the world around us.

## Contribution to the Formation of the State and the Role of the Ruler

Aristotle's political philosophy, outlined in *Politics*, is one of his most enduring contributions to human thought. He viewed the state as a natural institution arising from the human need for community and cooperation. For Aristotle, the polis (city-state) was the highest form of association, existing to promote the common good and enable its citizens to achieve their fullest potential.

**The Nature of the State:** Aristotle believed that human beings are inherently social creatures, famously stating, 'Man is by nature a political animal.' He argued that the state exists to achieve the highest form of human flourishing, or 'eudaimonia'. Unlike individual or familial associations, the state provides the structure necessary for cultivating virtues, ensuring justice and fostering a sense of belonging among its citizens.

**The Role of the Ruler:** Aristotle emphasized that the ruler's primary role is to govern in the interest of the community, not personal gain. In his classification of governments, he outlined three ideal forms of governance: monarchy, aristocracy and polity. However, he warned that these forms could degenerate into tyranny, oligarchy and mob rule, respectively, when rulers pursued selfish objectives.

The ideal ruler, according to Aristotle, is a philosopher-king, a wise and virtuous individual who prioritizes the welfare of the state and its people. He argued that governance should aim to strike a balance between the competing interests of different social classes, ensuring stability and justice. Aristotle's belief in a mixed government, combining elements of democracy, aristocracy and monarchy, is reflected in modern political systems, particularly constitutional democracies.

## The Middle Class as the Stabilizing Force

A groundbreaking aspect of Aristotle's political philosophy is his recognition of the middle class as the stabilizing force in any society. He asserted that extreme inequalities lead to instability and conflict, whereas a robust middle class promotes harmony and justice. His insights on economic equity and social balance remain relevant in contemporary political discourse.

## ANECDOTES

### 1. The Walking Philosopher

Aristotle founded the Lyceum, where he taught philosophy in a unique way – by walking around while lecturing. His students, called 'peripatetics' (Greek for 'walkers'), followed him as he debated and explained ideas.

This dynamic teaching style highlighted active engagement with knowledge and became a hallmark of Aristotelian education.

### 2. The Will of Aristotle

Unlike Plato, who believed in philosopher-kings, Aristotle had a practical approach to governance. Before his death, Aristotle wrote a detailed will, ensuring the well-being of his family, students and even his slaves. He also arranged for the continued functioning of the Lyceum.

This meticulous will reflects Aristotle's belief in rational planning and the ethical responsibility of individuals towards society.

### 3. Aristotle vs. Plato: The Rift

Although Aristotle studied under Plato for twenty years, he gradually disagreed with his mentor's Theory of Forms. He famously said, 'Plato is dear to me, but dearer still is the truth.' This marked a major philosophical shift – while Plato emphasized abstract ideals, Aristotle grounded his philosophy in empirical observation and the physical world.

### Why His Ideas Matter Today

Aristotle's ideas about the state, governance and citizenship have deeply influenced modern political thought. His emphasis on the rule of law, participatory governance and the moral responsibilities of rulers shaped the development of democratic principles. His theories informed the works of Enlightenment thinkers like John Locke and Montesquieu, laying the intellectual foundation for modern democratic constitutions.

Aristotle's categorization of governments and his analysis of power dynamics continue to guide political scientists and policymakers. His belief in the importance of education, civic virtue and community engagement resonates in contemporary debates on governance and public policy.

## MONTESQUIEU: THE ARCHITECT OF POLITICAL FREEDOM AND THE SEPARATION OF POWERS

### Historical Context and Introduction

Charles-Louis de Secondat, Baron de La Brède et de Montesquieu, was born on 18 January 1689 in La Brède, near

Bordeaux, France. He lived during the Age of Enlightenment, a transformative period when Europe was experiencing significant intellectual and cultural shifts. Thinkers of this era questioned traditional power structures, including absolute monarchy, and promoted individual rights and freedoms. Montesquieu's work was shaped by the political and social realities of eighteenth-century France, where autocracy and the centralized power of kings were beginning to face challenges from emerging ideas of democracy and governance. His theory of the separation of powers greatly influenced modern political thought, especially the US Constitution.

**Brief Biography**

Montesquieu was born into French nobility, inheriting the title of Baron de La Brède from his family. His father, a soldier, upheld the values of service and tradition while his mother, who died early in his childhood, left him a substantial inheritance. This privileged upbringing gave Montesquieu access to an excellent education and the means to pursue his intellectual interests.

His early life coincided with the reign of Louis XIV, whose policies centralized authority and strengthened the monarchy. While Versailles was a symbol of power and opulence, it was also a representation of inequality, with the lower classes burdened by taxation and the nobility growing increasingly disconnected from societal realities. Montesquieu's aristocratic status placed him in proximity to power, but he was acutely aware of the injustices and excesses of absolutist rule.

After completing his formal education, Montesquieu studied law in Bordeaux. Upon the death of his uncle, he inherited the title of baron and the position of president of the Parlement of Bordeaux. This role immersed him in the practicalities of governance and law enforcement, exposing him to the complexities and inadequacies of judicial processes under an absolute monarchy.

Montesquieu's education played a foundational role in shaping his philosophical outlook. He studied at the prestigious Collège de Juilly in Paris, where he gained a classical education steeped in Greek and Roman philosophy. Exposure to the works of Cicero, Tacitus and Aristotle gave him a historical perspective on governance, liberty and justice. Later, his readings of contemporary thinkers like John Locke further influenced his ideas about individual rights and the social contract.

His legal training provided Montesquieu with analytical skills and a practical understanding of the law's role in society. However, his most transformative influence came from his travels, particularly his time in England. Observing the constitutional monarchy in England, Montesquieu admired the balance of power between the monarchy, Parliament and the judiciary. This experience deeply influenced his later works, particularly his theory of the separation of powers.

The France of Montesquieu's time was marked by inequality, stagnation and the centralization of authority. The social structure was rigidly divided into the three estates: the clergy, nobility and commoners. While the nobility enjoyed privileges, they were often dependent on the king, whose absolute power dominated the political system.

Meanwhile, commoners faced oppressive taxes and limited opportunities for social mobility. This sociopolitical backdrop served as the impetus for Montesquieu's critiques.

His legal career exposed him to the injustices perpetrated by the system, and his writings became a platform to challenge these inequities. Montesquieu's work sought to reconcile the need for stability with the protection of individual liberties, proposing reforms that balanced authority and ensured justice.

He gained early fame with *The Persian Letters*, a satirical work that critiqued European society and politics. However, his most influential work, *The Spirit of Laws*, explored theories on government, law and political freedom. He advocated for a balanced government with checks and balances, which made him a key figure in the development of modern constitutionalism.

### Core Contribution to Political Philosophy

Montesquieu's most significant contribution to political philosophy is his theory of the 'separation of powers'. He argues that political power should not be concentrated in the hands of a single ruler or institution. His works reflect his deep understanding of governance and human society, and they remain cornerstones of modern democratic systems.

His key contributions and theories are:

**Theory of Separation of Powers:** Montesquieu introduced the idea that governmental power should be divided into the executive (to enforce laws), the legislative (to create laws), and the judiciary (to interpret laws). Each branch would check the others, preventing any one group from becoming too powerful, thereby ensuring individual freedom.

**Checks and Balances:** Building on the separation of powers, Montesquieu emphasized that each branch must have mechanisms to limit the others. He warned that unchecked power leads to oppression and advocated for a political system that balances authority and liberty.

**Adaptation of Laws to Society:** Montesquieu argued that laws should reflect the culture, geography and history of a society. He rejected the notion of universal governance models, insisting that good governance requires tailoring laws to specific contexts.

**Political Liberty and Justice:** He defined liberty as the ability to act within the law's bounds and advocated for governance structures that safeguard individual freedoms while maintaining order.

He also believed that different types of governments (republics, monarchies and despotisms) work best in different social and cultural contexts. For example, he suggested that republican governments are best suited for small states with virtuous citizens, while monarchies are better for large, complex societies.

Let us also look at some of his major works:

### *The Persian Letters* (1721)

Montesquieu's *The Persian Letters* is a satirical novel written as a series of letters between two fictional Persian travellers observing French society. Using this narrative device,

Montesquieu critiqued the absolutism of Louis XIV, religious intolerance and the rigid social structures of France.

He used the foreign perspectives of the Persian travellers to challenge European ethnocentrism and advocate for understanding diverse cultures. The book also critiqued the church's dominance and called for a more inclusive, tolerant approach to religion. And through satire, Montesquieu exposed the corruption, hypocrisy and inequality that characterized French society.

This work resonated with Enlightenment ideals by encouraging readers to question tradition and authority. Its popularity demonstrated the growing appetite for reform and set the stage for Montesquieu's later, more systemic critiques.

### *The Spirit of Laws* (1748)

This is one of the most significant contributions to political philosophy, distinguished by its depth, breadth and originality. Spanning thirty-one books, this magnum opus systematically examines governance, laws and their relationship with human societies. The book represents a synthesis of Montesquieu's empirical observations, historical study and philosophical reasoning, making it a foundation of modern political thought.

Montesquieu wrote *The Spirit of Laws* during a time when the absolutism of monarchs like Louis XIV had dominated Europe, suppressing liberty and centralizing power. The Enlightenment was just beginning to challenge these traditional structures, promoting ideas of reason, individual rights and governance reform. Montesquieu sought to understand and articulate the principles that sustain just and stable governments.

His legal training and experience as president of the Parlement of Bordeaux, which was a high court of justice during the Ancien Régime, serving the region of Guyenne in France, provided first-hand insight into the problems of arbitrary rule and judicial corruption.

Moreover, his admiration for the English constitutional monarchy, which he observed during his travels, inspired him to propose models of governance that balanced authority and protected liberty. *The Spirit of Laws* emerged as a response to these challenges and opportunities, blending Montesquieu's observations with his belief in the possibility of creating systems that prevent tyranny and promote justice.

The most revolutionary idea in *The Spirit of Laws* is Montesquieu's theory of the separation of powers, which underpins constitutional democracies today. He proposed that government power should be divided among three branches:

1. Legislative power: Responsible for creating laws
2. Executive power: Responsible for enforcing laws and managing the state
3. Judicial power: Responsible for interpreting laws and ensuring justice

Montesquieu believed that the concentration of power in a single authority, whether a monarch, an oligarchy or a democratic assembly, leads inevitably to tyranny. To safeguard liberty, he argued, these branches must be separate and independent, with mechanisms to check and balance each other. For example, the executive should have the power to veto legislative decisions while the judiciary must remain impartial and insulated from political pressures.

This idea was groundbreaking because it introduced a systematic way to limit authority and ensure accountability within government. The separation of powers formed the basis of the US Constitution and influenced constitutional designs worldwide. Even today, it remains essential for preventing authoritarianism and protecting individual freedoms in democratic systems.

Montesquieu famously wrote, 'When the legislative and executive powers are united in the same person or body, there can be no liberty... there is no liberty if the judiciary power is not separated from the legislative and executive.' This insight underscores the enduring relevance of his ideas as debates about checks and balances remain central to contemporary governance.

Montesquieu classified governments into three main types, based on their organizing principles:

1. Republics: Governed by the collective will of the people or their representatives. The core principle of republics is virtue, which Montesquieu defined as the active participation of citizens and their dedication to the public good. Republics could be further divided into democracies, where the people directly govern, and aristocracies, where governance is carried out by a select group.
2. Monarchies: Governed by a single ruler constrained by laws and institutions. Montesquieu believed monarchies were guided by honour, a concept that motivates individuals to act in the interest of the state through recognition and status.
3. Despotisms: Governed by a single ruler with absolute power. The principle of despotism is fear as the ruler maintains control through coercion and oppression.

Montesquieu saw this as the most dangerous form of government, prone to instability and injustice.

Montesquieu's classification was one of the earliest systematic analyses of governance based on principles rather than mere descriptions of regimes. By identifying the underlying forces that sustain each type of government, he provided a framework for understanding why some governments succeed while others fail. His focus on the psychological and cultural dimensions of governance (e.g., virtue, honour, and fear) added depth to the study of political systems, making *The Spirit of Laws* a pioneering text in political science.

While earlier thinkers like Aristotle and Machiavelli also categorized governments,

Montesquieu's approach was unique in linking governance types to human behaviour and societal principles. This relational model was revolutionary, laying the foundation for modern political sociology.

**Climate, Geography, Economy and Customs**

One of the most innovative aspects of his work is his relativistic approach, which argues that laws and governance must be tailored to the specific conditions of a society. He identified factors like climate, geography, economy and customs as crucial determinants of societal development and political structures.

1. Climate: Montesquieu believed that climate influences human behaviour, noting that people in warmer climates might be more lethargic due to environmental

factors, whereas those in colder climates might be more industrious. While this theory reflects the limitations of his era's scientific understanding, it demonstrates his attempt to integrate environmental considerations into political thought.

2. Geography: He observed that geography shapes economic activities, trade and political organization. For example, maritime nations like England develop differently from landlocked ones due to their reliance on commerce and naval power.
3. Economy: Montesquieu recognized the importance of economic structures in shaping governance. He emphasized the interplay between wealth distribution and political stability, foreshadowing later economic theories in political science.
4. Customs and traditions: He argued that societal norms and values must inform governance. Imposing laws without accounting for a society's customs leads to unrest and failure.

Montesquieu's relativistic approach was ahead of its time. While philosophers like Aristotle acknowledged the role of geography in governance, Montesquieu expanded this idea into a comprehensive framework that integrated multiple societal factors. His emphasis on environmental and cultural determinants influenced later thinkers like Alexis de Tocqueville and Max Weber.

**Liberty as a Balance between Freedom and Security**

Montesquieu defined liberty not as unlimited freedom but as the ability to act within the law's constraints to ensure collective security. For Montesquieu, true liberty exists only when individuals are protected from arbitrary rule, and this requires a balance between personal freedom and the government's authority to maintain order.

Having witnessed the abuses of absolutist regimes, Montesquieu understood that unchecked freedom leads to chaos while unchecked authority leads to oppression. His balanced conception of liberty reflects his belief in moderation and the rule of law as essential for justice and stability.

This idea remains vital in contemporary political discourse as governments worldwide grapple with balancing individual rights and collective security in areas like surveillance, public health and counterterrorism. Montesquieu's insights remind us that liberty cannot flourish without institutional safeguards that protect citizens from both anarchy and despotism.

## ANECDOTES

### 1. Montesquieu's Visit to England

During his travels to England in the 1720s, Montesquieu observed the constitutional monarchy and was impressed by the balance of power between the monarchy, Parliament and judiciary. He studied how these institutions worked together to safeguard liberty.

Montesquieu's admiration for the English system led directly to his theory of the separation of powers. He remarked, 'England is the nation which enjoys the most liberty,' recognizing that balanced governance is key to protecting individual freedoms.

### 2. *The Spirit of Laws* and the US Constitution

Although Montesquieu never visited the United States, his ideas became a cornerstone of its founding principles. James Madison and Alexander Hamilton cited *The Spirit of Laws* extensively during the drafting of the US Constitution, particularly regarding the separation of powers and checks and balances.

Montesquieu's influence on the US Constitution highlights his enduring legacy. His ideas transcended national boundaries, shaping democratic institutions worldwide.

### Why His Ideas Matter Today

Montesquieu's theories on the separation of powers and checks and balances remain fundamental to modern democratic governance. His ideas directly influenced the US Constitution, shaping the division of government into three branches to prevent tyranny and ensure accountability. His emphasis on the role of law in protecting liberty and his criticism of absolute monarchy continue to resonate in contemporary debates on state power and civil liberties.

As a foundation of political science and constitutional law, Montesquieu's insights into the relationship between laws, society and government remain highly relevant. His belief that laws should be adapted to cultural, geographic and economic contexts influences ongoing discussions on governance, international law and human rights.

In an era of rising authoritarianism and democratic erosion, Montesquieu's warnings about the corrupting nature of power and the need for institutional safeguards are more crucial than ever. His relativistic approach to governance underscores the importance of tailoring political systems to the unique needs of societies, ensuring their adaptability across diverse contexts.

Montesquieu was a visionary thinker who challenged entrenched authority and laid the foundation for modern political philosophy. Through works like *The Persian Letters* and *The Spirit of Laws*, he demonstrated how intellectual rigour could uncover principles for lasting governance. His legacy endures as a guiding force for justice, liberty and balanced power structures – reminding us of the need to protect individual freedoms, foster accountability and continuously adapt governance to meet the evolving challenges of humanity.

## VOLTAIRE: THE ADVOCATE OF FREEDOM, TOLERANCE AND REASON

### Historical Context and Introduction

François-Marie Arouet, known by his pen name Voltaire, was born on 21 November 1694 in Paris during the Enlightenment, a time focused on reason, individual rights and critical thinking. Voltaire lived through the tumultuous times of absolute monarchies and oppressive church doctrines, particularly in France, where political and religious power were closely intertwined.

Voltaire became an emblem of this transformative age, championing ideals that catalysed major sociopolitical revolutions. The Enlightenment, which sought to challenge superstition and champion individual freedoms, found in Voltaire one of its most articulate and fearless advocates.

His sharp critiques of religious intolerance, absolutism and social injustice made him an influential Enlightenment thinker. His works laid the intellectual foundations for the French Revolution and influenced the liberal democracies that emerged thereafter.

**Brief Biography**

Voltaire's early years were marked by contrasts – a privileged education juxtaposed against frequent clashes with authority. Born into a middle-class family, he received a rigourous classical education at the Jesuit Collège Louis-le-Grand in Paris. Here, his sharp intellect and love for literature flourished, but his rebellious spirit also emerged. Instead of pursuing a conventional path in law, as his father intended, Voltaire sought a life in letters.

His first major clash with authority occurred in 1717 when he was imprisoned in the Bastille for his satirical writings about the French monarchy. The incident was sparked by Voltaire's composition of defamatory verses directed at the regent, Philippe II, Duke of Orléans. The verses ridiculed the regent's personal life and governance, crossing a line even for the relatively permissive literary culture of the time.

While imprisoned for eleven months, Voltaire began work on *Oedipe*, his first successful play. This period in the Bastille marked a turning point in his life: far from being cowed, Voltaire emerged more determined to wield his pen against social injustice and abuses of power. He wrote plays, novels, essays and historical works. His outspoken views on religion, politics and society often led to controversy, imprisonment and exile.

Voltaire's intellectual journey was largely shaped by self-education despite his classical training at the Jesuit Collège Louis-le-Grand. He displayed an insatiable curiosity and a willingness to explore ideas beyond the constraints of formal pedagogy. His exposure to the works of John Locke and Isaac Newton, two towering figures of the Enlightenment, was pivotal in his development.

Voltaire embraced Locke's empiricism, which highlighted the role of human experience in shaping understanding. Locke's views on the social contract, the right to individual freedom and the separation of church and state deeply influenced Voltaire's political outlook.

Voltaire also greatly admired Newton's capacity to unify complex phenomena under universal principles. Their ideas collectively underscored the power of rationality, observation and scepticism, which Voltaire synthesized into his worldview, positioning himself as a bridge between scientific inquiry and humanistic thought.

His most famous works include *Candide*, *Letters on England* and *Philosophical Dictionary*. Voltaire was a passionate advocate for civil liberties, particularly freedom of speech, freedom of religion and the separation of church and state. His wit, satirical style and fearless critiques of established institutions earned him both admiration and criticism in equal measure.

### Core Contribution to Political Philosophy

Voltaire's political philosophy centred on the ideas of individual liberty, freedom of expression and religious tolerance. He was a vocal critic of the French monarchy and the Catholic Church, seeing them as corrupt and oppressive forces. One of Voltaire's most enduring contributions to political thought is his advocacy for secularism, or the separation of religion from government, which he argued was necessary for both political freedom and intellectual progress.

## A Master of Satire and Philosophy

Voltaire's choice of satire as his primary literary vehicle was deliberate and strategic. Living in an era where censorship was rampant and dissent often met with persecution, satire allowed Voltaire to veil his criticisms of power structures in humour and allegory, making them palatable to a broader audience.

Satire also served as a means to distill complex philosophical concepts into narratives that were accessible to both the intellectual elite and the general public. For example, in *Candide*, Voltaire critiques Leibnizian optimism – a highly abstract philosophical doctrine – by weaving it into the absurd misadventures of his protagonist. Through humour and irony, Voltaire exposed the dangers of blind faith in abstract theories while advocating for practical wisdom and resilience.

Voltaire also used satire to disarm his critics. His sharp wit made him a formidable opponent as he could reduce grandiose ideas or powerful figures to objects of ridicule. By presenting his critiques with a light-hearted veneer, Voltaire made his radical ideas more difficult to suppress and more likely to resonate with his readers.

### *Candide*

One of Voltaire's most influential works is *Candide* (1759), a satirical novella that exemplifies his mastery of blending sharp wit with profound philosophical criticism. The novella challenges the optimistic philosophy espoused by Leibniz, who argued that 'this is the best of all possible worlds'. Through *Candide*'s journey, he illustrated the absurdity of this belief and the need for a rational, pragmatic approach to the world. Through humour, irony and absurdity, Voltaire dismantles this notion, exposing the dangers of complacency and uncritical acceptance of suffering. He also famously condemned religious dogmas and the clergy's abuse of power, advocating for a more tolerant and reasonable approach to faith. Voltaire's famous slogan 'Écrasez l'infâ me' (crush the infamous thing) referred to his fight against religious intolerance, superstition and injustices in the name of religion. Voltaire argued for a legal system that protects individual rights and a government that respects personal freedoms. He believed that reason should guide society's progress.

He employed several key themes and techniques in *Candide* that elevate it as a cornerstone of satirical political literature:

- Critique of Optimism: The character Pangloss, *Candide's* mentor, represents the absurdity of Leibnizian optimism. His repeated assertion that all is for the best, even in the face of calamity, is a biting satire on the dangers of philosophical naïveté.
- Religious Hypocrisy: Voltaire uses *Candide* to expose the moral failings of religious institutions. By highlighting the greed, corruption and cruelty of clergy members, he critiques the gap between their preaching and actions.
- Human Suffering: Dark humour pervades the novella, with Voltaire portraying human suffering in a way that is both sobering and absurd. This approach underscores the need for realistic, compassionate responses to life's challenges rather than passive acceptance.
- 'We must cultivate our garden': The novella's famous closing line encapsulates Voltaire's pragmatic philosophy. It advocates for practical action and personal responsibility, encouraging individuals to

focus on improving their immediate circumstances and communities.

### Contribution to Satirical Political Literature

Beyond *Candide*, Voltaire's broader body of work represents a significant contribution to satirical political literature. His use of wit and irony allowed him to rebuke the power structures of his time – monarchies, organized religion and societal hierarchies – without falling victim to the same dogmatic rigidity he opposed.

In works such as *Letters on the English*, Voltaire explores political and cultural contrasts between England and France, subtly advocating for constitutional monarchy and religious tolerance. This comparative satire became a vehicle for introducing revolutionary ideas to his French readership, challenging the absolutism of the Ancien Régime.

Voltaire's *Philosophical Dictionary* is another notable example. Through a series of essays disguised as entries, he criticizes everything from religious dogma to entrenched traditions. This work exemplifies his ability to combine humour, intellectual depth and political commentary, making intricate ideas accessible to a wide audience.

His legacy in satirical political literature lies in his ability to weaponize humour as a tool for reform. Voltaire's writings reveal the power of satire to inspire critical thinking, expose duplicity and ignite social and political change.

### Criticism of the Catholic Church

Voltaire's disparagement of the Catholic Church was one of the defining features of his career. He saw the Church not only as a spiritual institution but also as a political power that perpetuated ignorance, inequality and oppression. His attacks on the Church were rooted in his broader Enlightenment ideals of reason, tolerance and individual liberty.

One of Voltaire's central grievances was the Church's role in stifling intellectual freedom. Through censorship, the Inquisition and its alliance with absolutist monarchies, the Church wielded immense power over thought and expression. Voltaire viewed this as antithetical to the pursuit of knowledge and progress. His criticism was not limited to dogma; he condemned the Church's wealth, corruption and hypocrisy, contrasting its opulence with the poverty of the masses it claimed to serve.

The effects of Voltaire's censure were profound. In the short term, his works fuelled debates about the relationship between religion and the state, contributing to the decline of ecclesiastical authority in Europe. His ideas inspired movements towards secular governance and the eventual separation of church and state in many parts of the Western world.

Globally, Voltaire's insistence on religious tolerance and freedom of thought resonated far beyond Europe. His advocacy for deism and his critiques of institutional religion laid the intellectual groundwork for modern debates on the role of religion in public life. By challenging the Church's monopoly on morality, Voltaire opened the door to pluralism, rational ethics and the emergence of secular humanism.

## ANECDOTES

### 1. Exile to England

After an altercation with a nobleman, Voltaire was exiled to England, a pivotal moment in his intellectual journey.

There, he encountered a society that valued political freedom, religious tolerance and scientific progress.

Voltaire's philosophy was deeply inspired by the works of Locke and Newton during his time in England. His *Letters on the English* (1733) praised the country's advancements while exposing the shortcomings of French absolutism. The book was banned in France, but it cemented Voltaire's role as a sharp critic of authoritarian rule.

### 2. The Ferney Years

After years of exile and persecution, Voltaire settled in Ferney, near the French–Swiss border, where he transformed his estate into a hub of intellectual activity. Ferney became a refuge for thinkers, artists and dissidents, earning Voltaire a reputation as an enlightened patriarch.

From this stronghold, he launched relentless campaigns against religious intolerance and injustice, including his famous interventions in wrongful conviction cases like that of Jean Calas. His activism at Ferney solidified his legacy as both a philosopher and a defender of human rights.

### Why His Ideas Matter Today

Voltaire's ideas on free speech, religious tolerance and secularism shaped modern liberal democracies. His work paved the way for the development of constitutional rights and the idea that individuals should freely express themselves and practise their faith without fear of government persecution. His call for tolerance remains relevant in debates about religion, freedom of speech and the government's role in public life.

Voltaire's emphasis on reason, scepticism of authority, and intellectual freedom still applies today. His legacy endures in the ongoing struggles for human rights and social justice worldwide.

## JEAN-JACQUES ROUSSEAU: THE CHAMPION OF DEMOCRACY AND THE SOCIAL CONTRACT

### Historical Context and Introduction

Jean-Jacques Rousseau was born in 1712 in Geneva, Switzerland, a small Protestant city-state known for its unique blend of republican governance and religious orthodoxy. Geneva's political structure valued civic participation but maintained significant social hierarchies, a contradiction that shaped Rousseau's later critiques of inequality.

Rousseau lived during the Enlightenment, a period of intellectual upheaval emphasizing reason, science and progress. However, he stood apart from contemporaries like Voltaire and Diderot by questioning whether such progress genuinely improved human morality and happiness.

He was troubled by the contradiction that while liberty and equality were praised, power and privilege dominated society. His work challenged the established order, offering new ideas about human nature, society and the government. Rousseau's ideas would go on to inspire revolutionary movements and influence modern political thought, especially in the context of democracy and social justice.

### Brief Biography

Rousseau came from a middle-class family and had a difficult childhood. His formative years were shaped by personal tragedies, social displacement and early exposure to oppression. His mother died shortly after his birth, and he had an estranged relationship with his father, who fled Geneva when Rousseau was just ten, leaving him under the care of relatives.

Rousseau was apprenticed to an engraver, who subjected him to harsh treatment, including physical abuse and demeaning tasks. This experience fuelled his later disdain for oppressive hierarchies and exploitation.

At sixteen, Rousseau fled Geneva, wandering through Switzerland and France. He took various jobs as a servant, secretary and music teacher while educating himself through voracious reading. Those years of poverty and exposure to privilege shaped his empathy for the marginalized.

Rousseau's intellectual journey was driven by his self-directed studies of classical and contemporary thinkers.

Plato's *Republic* presented an ideal society where justice and the common good prevail over individual desires. Rousseau absorbed this vision, adapting it into his concept of the general will.

Montaigne's essays emphasized personal reflection and experiential learning, challenging rigid educational traditions. Rousseau expanded on these principles in *Émile,* advocating for natural education, where children learn through experiences that align with their natural curiosity.

Locke's *Some Thoughts Concerning Education* introduced him to the concept of tabula rasa (blank slate), proposing that children are born without pre-existing ideas and develop knowledge through experience. While Locke focused on reason, Rousseau added a moral dimension, asserting that children are innately good and corrupted by societal influences. This belief underpins his argument in *The Social*

*Contract* that societal structures, not human nature, are the root of inequality.

Rousseau's patron, intellectual guide, and later, his lover, Madame de Warens was a wealthy and independent woman, whom he met in Savoy after fleeing Geneva. She introduced him to Enlightenment ideas, music and the aristocratic lifestyle, shaping his intellectual foundation. Their complex relationship, blending maternal care and romantic involvement, deeply influenced Rousseau's emotional and philosophical development.

Though the relationship ended after several years, Madame de Warens's influence is evident in Rousseau's early works, particularly his emphasis on individuality and natural harmony. Despite limited formal education, he became one of the most influential thinkers of the Enlightenment. Controversial in his time, Rousseau was often at odds with other Enlightenment thinkers and political leaders. His views on the role of the state, the general will and the corrupting influence of civilization made him both revered and reviled in equal measure.

## Core Contribution to Political Philosophy

Rousseau's biggest idea was *The Social Contract*, which argued that legitimate political authority comes from an agreement among people to form a society. He believed that humans were originally free and equal, but private property and social institutions created inequality and oppression.

### *The Social Contract*

Written in 1762, it arose from Rousseau's desire to address the moral and political crises of his time. Living in exile and reflecting on the injustices of feudalism, he sought to reconcile individual freedom with collective governance.

Core Question: How can individuals remain free while living under the rule of law?

Rousseau's answer was the concept of a social contract, a voluntary agreement forming the foundation of legitimate political authority.

Rousseau begins with: 'Man is born free, and everywhere he is in chains.' He argues that natural liberty is lost in society, but it can be reclaimed through a social contract and when individuals collectively agree to laws that embody the general will. It represents the collective good, guiding laws and policies. Laws aligned with the general will ensure freedom and equality. For Rousseau, individuals obeying self-imposed laws under the social contract achieve true freedom. He further examined different governance systems, advocating for direct democracy in small states while acknowledging that larger societies require representation. He believed a shared civic faith is essential for social unity. Rousseau denounced institutionalized religion for dividing loyalties.

While widely celebrated for its egalitarian vision, Rousseau's belief in the innate goodness of humanity has been slammed as overly idealistic. Critics argue that his reliance on collective morality risks suppressing individual freedoms.

## Influence on the French Revolution and Political Philosophy

The French Revolution (1789–99) was a period of profound social, political and economic upheaval in France that dismantled the monarchy, ended feudal privileges and established revolutionary ideals of liberty, equality and fraternity. To understand Rousseau's influence, it is essential to grasp the historical context leading up to the Revolution.

By the late eighteenth century, France faced mounting debt due to wars and extravagant royal spending, including the construction of Versailles. King Louis XVI's inability to manage the economy led to widespread discontent. The tax system disproportionately burdened the Third Estate (commoners), while the clergy and nobility enjoyed privileges.

French society was divided into three estates: the First Estate: clergy; the Second Estate, nobility; and the Third Estate, commoners (over 95 per cent of the population), who were heavily taxed and excluded from political power, fuelling resentment.

Enlightenment thinkers like Rousseau, Voltaire and Montesquieu challenged the divine right of kings, advocated for individual rights and laid emphasis on reason. Rousseau's critique of inequality and his ideas on popular sovereignty were particularly influential.

In 1789, the Estates-General was convened to address the financial crisis but devolved into disputes over representation. The Third Estate declared itself the National Assembly, initiating a series of events leading to the Revolution.

Rousseau's ideas permeated the Revolution at multiple stages, guiding revolutionary leaders and shaping their vision of a new society.

**1789.** The Beginning of the Revolution: The National Assembly's creation and the storming of the Bastille marked the Revolution's start. The Third Estate's call for equality and representation echoed Rousseau's critique of feudal hierarchies in *Discourse on Inequality*.

**1791.** The Constitution of 1791: France became a constitutional monarchy. However, tensions remained between radicals and moderates. The idea of popular sovereignty in *The Social Contract* inspired demands for more democratic reforms, leading to calls for a republic.

**1792.** The Establishment of the First French Republic: The monarchy was abolished, and the First French Republic was declared. Revolutionary leaders like Maximilien Robespierre drew heavily from Rousseau's works. Robespierre, known as 'The Incorruptible', was a staunch admirer of Rousseau, calling *The Social Contract* 'the gospel of civic virtue'. He adopted Rousseau's concept of the general will to justify policies aimed at achieving collective equality.

**1793–94.** The Reign of Terror: During this period, the Jacobins, led by Robespierre, used the general will to justify extreme measures, including mass executions of perceived enemies of the Revolution. While Rousseau envisioned the general will as a democratic tool, the Jacobins used it to justify authoritarian control, leading to criticism of Rousseau's ideas as potentially dangerous when misapplied.

**1799.** The End of the Revolution: The Revolution ended with Napoleon Bonaparte's rise to power. Although Napoleon established authoritarian rule, he retained some revolutionary ideals inspired by Rousseau, including legal equality and civic participation.

**Key Revolutionary Leaders Influenced by Rousseau**

- Maximilien Robespierre: His belief in civic virtue and his justification for the Reign of Terror were rooted in Rousseau's *The Social Contract*. However, his authoritarian interpretation of the general will led to significant controversy.

- Jean-Paul Marat: A radical journalist and revolutionary, Marat cited Rousseau's critiques of inequality to rally the common people against aristocratic privilege.
- Georges Danton: Danton, a more moderate revolutionary leader, used Rousseau's principles to advocate for legal reforms and social equality.

**Rousseau's Enduring Influence on Political Philosophy**

Beyond the French Revolution, Rousseau's ideas became foundational to modern political thought. Rousseau's belief that legitimate authority arises from the consent of the governed influenced democratic movements worldwide. His ideas inspired later philosophers like Karl Marx, John Rawls, and even Gandhi, who echoed Rousseau's emphasis on collective welfare.

His analysis of private property in *Discourse on Inequality* laid the groundwork for debates on socialism and economic justice. His call for a unifying civil religion to strengthen social cohesion influenced discussions on the relationship between religion and state.

In *Discourse on Inequality*, Rousseau traced social disparity to private property and artificial hierarchies. *The Social Contract* and *Émile* together formed a vision of governance and education that stressed moral equality and collective freedom.

While celebrated for his egalitarian vision, Rousseau's concept of the general will has been panned for its potential to justify authoritarianism. Detractors argue that prioritizing the collective good can suppress individual freedoms, as seen during the Jacobin dictatorship.

### *Émile*: A Revolutionary Approach to Education

Published in 1762, *Émile* proposed a radical educational model grounded in children's natural development. Core principles that were proposed in the book include:

- Education should nurture children's innate curiosity and moral instincts.
- Teachers should act as guides, allowing children to learn through experience rather than rigid instruction.

Across five books, the text explores human development from infancy to adulthood. Book I emphasizes how infants learn through sensory exploration, while Book II highlights the role of play and discovery in fostering reasoning during childhood. Book III focuses on adolescence, where practical skills and independence take centre stage. Book IV shifts to moral education, stressing the importance of empathy and civic responsibility. However, Book V is controversial as it advocates gendered education, promoting traditional roles for women.

## ANECDOTES

### 1. *The Social Contract* and the French Revolution

Decades after Rousseau's death, *The Social Contract* became a revolutionary scripture. Robespierre and the Jacobins invoked its principles to justify radical reforms during the French Revolution. However, its misinterpretation led to extreme measures during the Reign of Terror, illustrating the dangers of applying philosophical ideas dogmatically. Rousseau had envisioned a society based on collective will, but he could hardly have foreseen the bloodshed carried out in its name.

### 2. A Philosopher's Tomb Turned Pilgrimage Site

After being enshrined in the Panthéon, Rousseau's tomb became a pilgrimage site for revolutionaries and intellectuals alike. Visitors saw him as the philosopher who championed equality and popular sovereignty. His posthumous journey from exile to the heart of France's national memory mirrored the transformation of his ideas – from radical to revered to reinterpreted across centuries.

### Why His Ideas Matter Today

Jean-Jacques Rousseau's theories on democracy, equality and the role of the state continue to shape contemporary debates on social justice and political authority. His concept of the general will laid the foundation for democratic systems, accentuating popular sovereignty and participatory governance. His critiques of inequality and property inspired socialist and egalitarian movements, influencing modern discussions on economic and social justice.

Beyond politics, Rousseau's views on education and moral development remain influential, particularly in child-centred learning approaches that prioritize individuality and autonomy. His belief in experiential education continues to mould modern pedagogical practices.

In today's world, where tensions between individual rights and collective responsibility persist, Rousseau's idea that true freedom emerges from commitment to the common good serves as a powerful guiding principle. His legacy endures in movements advocating for democracy, equality and sustainability, reminding us of the need to balance personal liberty with social responsibility. Despite criticism, Rousseau's vision challenges us to build a more just, inclusive and compassionate world.

## IMMANUEL KANT: THE PHILOSOPHER OF DUTY AND UNIVERSAL ETHICS

### Historical Context and Introduction

Immanuel Kant was born in 1724 in Königsberg (now Kaliningrad, Russia) during the Age of Enlightenment.

The scientific breakthroughs of Isaac Newton inspired a generation of thinkers to apply similar universal laws to ethics, society and politics. Kant emerged from this intellectual milieu, determined to establish a rational framework for understanding the human experience. His work marked a key shift in philosophy as he aimed to connect the Enlightenment ideals of individual freedom, rational governance and equality. Kant explored how people understand the world and make ethical choices, shaping modern ideas on ethics, metaphysics and knowledge.

### Brief Biography

Kant was the fourth of nine children in a modest Pietist household. Pietism, a Protestant movement, emphasized personal piety, simplicity and a direct relationship with god, prioritizing moral action over ritual. This upbringing instilled in Kant a strong sense of duty and discipline, which became the bedrock of his later ethical theories.

At sixteen, Kant enrolled at the University of Königsberg to study theology. However, his curiosity soon led him to mathematics, physics and philosophy. This shift reflected the Enlightenment's belief in the power of multidisciplinary learning. For instance, his engagement with physics underpinned his later exploration of causality while his study of mathematics informed his methodical philosophical system.

Kant's transition from theology to secular studies was influenced by the intellectual trends of his time, particularly the tension between faith and reason. He sought to reconcile these domains, believing that a universal moral framework could emerge from rational inquiry.

Kant spent most of his life in Königsberg, where he taught philosophy as well. His intellectual journey was influenced by thinkers like René Descartes, David Hume and Leibniz. His most influential works include *Critique of Pure Reason*, *Critique of Practical Reason* and *Groundwork of the Metaphysics of Morals*. These books introduced his theories on knowledge, morality and human freedom. His philosophy challenged traditional views on metaphysics and ethics, and his work remains central to philosophy today.

### Core Contribution to Political Philosophy

Kant's political ideas are linked to his moral philosophy, especially the categorical imperative. This principle states that people should act only in ways that could become universal laws. In politics, this means respecting the rights and dignity of all individuals, treating them as ends rather than as means.

In his essay 'Perpetual Peace', Kant argued that lasting peace is possible if nations form a federation of free republics. He imagined a world where states cooperate under just laws, guided by human rights. He believed true political freedom is not just the absence of restrictions but the organization of society around universal moral principles.

Kant also introduced the idea of a republican state, where laws are made through representative democracy and based on rational principles. He believed people have the right to self-governance and should help create the laws that govern them.

**Kant's Magnum Opus: *Critique of Pure Reason***

Kant's *Critique of Pure Reason* (1781) is a foundational work that addresses the scope and limitations of human understanding. It bridges metaphysics, ethics and epistemology, offering philosophical insights into how we experience and interpret the world. The central themes include phenomena, noumena, autonomy and active cognition.

**Phenomena and Noumena:** He distinguishes between the phenomena, that is the world as we perceive it, and the noumena, that is, the things-in-themselves, which exist independently of perception. For example, a tree as we see it (phenomena) is shaped by our senses and cognitive categories, but the tree as it exists (noumena) remains unknowable. This distinction underscores the limits of human knowledge, stressing that reality is filtered through our mental faculties.

**Autonomy:** Kant's notion of autonomy extends beyond ethics to encompass human cognition. Autonomy means self-governance, both morally and intellectually. For instance, in ethics, Kant argues that individuals must legislate their own moral laws, guided by reason rather than external authority. This principle laid the groundwork for democratic ideals, where citizens are viewed as rational agents capable of self-rule.

**Active Cognition:** Kant's revolutionary claim that the mind actively organizes sensory data challenges the traditional view of knowledge as a passive reception of facts. For example, categories like causality and space are not derived from the external world but are innate structures of the mind. This insight empowered Enlightenment thinkers to champion human agency in shaping not only knowledge but also society and politics.

Through the *Critique of Pure Reason*, Kant provided the philosophical tools to reconcile science, morality and metaphysics, influencing everything from epistemology to political theory.

**The Copernican Revolution: Origins, Naming and Impact**

Kant's 'Copernican Revolution' in philosophy marked a paradigm shift in understanding knowledge and reality. Inspired by Nicolaus Copernicus, who reversed the understanding of celestial motion by placing the sun at the centre, Kant proposed a similar inversion in philosophy: the mind actively shapes experience, rather than passively receiving information. This shift challenged both empiricism (e.g., Hume, who held that knowledge arises purely from experience) and rationalism (e.g., Leibniz, who relied solely on reason).

Kant named it the Copernican Revolution to highlight its transformative nature, placing human cognition at the centre of philosophical inquiry. He sought to resolve long-standing epistemological conflicts by asserting that objects conform to the mind's categories, such as time, space and causality.

The Copernican Revolution empowered individuals by highlighting their role as active agents in shaping knowledge. This extended to politics, where Kant argued for autonomy and moral responsibility as the basis for governance. For example, his ideas influenced the development of modern liberal democracy, where citizens are recognized as rational beings capable of participating in self-governance. The principle of active agency also resonates in contemporary movements advocating for human rights and social justice, where individual dignity and participation are paramount.

## The Categorical Imperative and Its Sociopolitical Influence

The categorical imperative is the foundation of Kant's moral philosophy. It is a universal principle that asserts:

1. Moral actions must be universally applicable.
2. Humans must always be treated as ends in themselves, not as means to an end.

Kant provides several formulations of the categorical imperative, one being the universalizability test: 'An action is moral only if it can be applied as a universal law.' For instance, lying is immoral because if everyone lied, trust would collapse. Another formulation stresses respecting individuals' dignity and autonomy, which is why Kant opposed practices like slavery as they reduced humans to mere tools.

The categorical imperative inspired the principles of equality, justice and individual rights in political philosophy. Kant's emphasis on treating individuals as ends informed the abolitionist movement and early human rights frameworks. It also laid the ethical foundation for democratic governance, where laws must reflect universal moral principles.

In modern politics, the categorical imperative underpins global human rights doctrines, such as the United Nations' Universal Declaration of Human Rights, which enshrines dignity and equality as universal values.

### Connecting Metaphysics to Politics

Kant believed that metaphysics provided the moral and rational foundations necessary for just governance. His political philosophy integrates metaphysical principles, such as autonomy and universal moral laws, into practical frameworks for society.

Kant's essay, 'Perpetual Peace: A Philosophical Sketch', outlines his vision of a cosmopolitan federation of states governed by reason and law. He argued that a rational political order must reflect universal moral laws, ensuring justice and equality. For instance, he proposed that perpetual peace could be achieved through international cooperation and the rule of law, principles that influenced the formation of the League of Nations and the United Nations.

Kant's vision is evident in contemporary global institutions like the UN, which strive for international peace through dialogue and cooperation. His stress on universal morality also echoes in debates over climate change, where nations are called upon to act collectively for the common good. 'The Paris Agreement', with its focus on shared responsibility, reflects Kantian ideals of global justice and moral duty.

Additionally, Kant's emphasis on autonomy informs modern democratic systems, where citizens are viewed as rational agents who contribute to shaping just laws. His ideas continue to inspire movements for social justice, such as the fight against systemic inequalities, where dignity and equality are central demands.

### Why His Ideas Matter Today

Kant's moral philosophy remains a cornerstone of modern ethics, particularly in discussions about human rights and justice. His highlighting of universal moral principles and respect for human dignity has had a profound effect on liberal political theory and international relations. Kant's idea of a peaceful republican world order continues to inspire debates about global governance, international law and human rights.

His concept of autonomy, that is, acting in accordance with universal moral laws that one gives to oneself, is central to contemporary discussions on personal freedom and the ethical responsibilities of individuals and governments. His vision of perpetual peace resonates in efforts to address global challenges like climate change and conflict resolution.

## ANECDOTES

### 1. Kant and Rousseau: A Portrait of Influence

Kant famously kept a portrait of Jean-Jacques Rousseau in his study, a symbol of the French philosopher's profound impact on his thinking. Despite being known for his rationalist approach, Kant was deeply moved by Rousseau's emphasis on human dignity, moral autonomy and the social contract. Rousseau's ideas led Kant to rethink the role of reason in ethics, culminating in his concept of the 'categorical imperative', which asserts that moral laws must be universal and self-imposed.

### 2. The Delayed Masterpiece

Kant spent over a decade refining *Critique of Pure Reason*, struggling with the complexity of his arguments and his desire for absolute clarity. He delayed publishing until he was satisfied that his work provided a rigourous foundation for metaphysics, epistemology and ethics.

This relentless pursuit of precision defined his approach to philosophy. The book eventually revolutionized modern thought, bridging the gap between rationalism and empiricism and laying the groundwork for nineteenth and twentieth-century philosophy.

## GEORG WILHELM FRIEDRICH HEGEL: THE PHILOSOPHER OF HISTORY AND REALITY

### Historical Context and Introduction

Hegel was born in 1770 in Stuttgart, Germany. He lived through major historical events of the late eighteenth and early nineteenth centuries, including the French Revolution and Napoleon's rise to power.

The Holy Roman Empire was a fragmented feudal system, weakened by internal conflicts and external pressures. Its dissolution in 1806 by Napoleon Bonaparte symbolized the rise of modern nation-states, a key theme in Hegel's philosophy of the state and history.

Hegel admired the Revolution's ideals of liberty, equality and fraternity, viewing it as a turning point in humanity's quest for freedom. However, the subsequent Reign of Terror (1793–94) highlighted the dangers of unrestrained liberty, reinforcing Hegel's belief in the need for order and rationality in governance. Hegel interpreted the Revolution as a dialectical process, freedom (thesis) clashing with tyranny (antithesis), eventually synthesizing into constitutional governance.

Hegel famously referred to Napoleon Bonaparte (1769–1821) as the 'world spirit on horseback', embodying the rational progression of history. Napoleon's reforms across Europe, including the abolition of feudal privileges, resonated with Hegel's vision of historical progress.

The Industrial Revolution (1760–1840) transformed Europe, creating contradictions between technological advancement and social inequality. Hegel's philosophy highlighted resolving such contradictions as essential to progress.

Hegel explored big questions about human freedom, historical progress and reality. His ideas influenced many fields, including political philosophy, history and theology.

## Brief Biography

Hegel's early life was shaped by his Protestant upbringing, which stressed ethics, discipline and the unity of faith and reason. His father, a civil servant, provided him with an understanding of bureaucratic systems that would later influence his views on governance.

From 1788 to 1793, Hegel studied at the Tübinger Stift, a Protestant seminary, where he formed pivotal friendships with the likes of Friedrich Hölderlin, a Romantic poet and philosopher, who introduced him to the ideals of the French Revolution and the philosophy of the ancient Greeks, and Friedrich Schelling, a fellow philosopher who shared Hegel's early fascination with German idealism, though later, they became rivals. Hölderlin's Romanticism and Schelling's speculative philosophy profoundly shaped Hegel's early works, too. Hegel's formative years were also marked by personal challenges, including the death of his mother in 1783. His readings during this time included the works of Immanuel Kant (1724–1804), whose critical philosophy inspired Hegel's interest in reconciling reason and metaphysics.

Hegel studied theology and philosophy, eventually becoming a professor at the University of Jena. Early in his career, he wrote about the dialectical method and history. His philosophy represents the peak of German Idealism, which explores the relationship between the mind and reality. His most influential works, *The Phenomenology of Spirit* and *The Philosophy of Right*, shaped the development of later thinkers, including Marxists and existentialists.

After completing his studies in theology in 1793, Hegel worked as a private tutor in Bern and Frankfurt, immersing himself in political and philosophical texts. These years allowed him to refine his ideas about freedom, ethics and the role of religion in society.

## Core Contribution to Political Philosophy

Hegel's political philosophy is centred on the idea of the 'absolute spirit' and the process of historical development. Hegel believed history follows a rational process, moving forward through contradictions (thesis and antithesis) that resolve into a higher understanding (synthesis).

His early writings included explorations of religion and morality. He critiqued the separation of faith and reason, arguing for their unity as a foundation for ethical life. He began to conceptualize the state as a rational and ethical entity, a theme he would later develop in *The Philosophy of Right*.

## *The Phenomenology of Spirit* (1807): A Masterpiece

Hegel's *The Phenomenology of Spirit* marked his emergence as a groundbreaking thinker. The book examines the evolution of human consciousness through a 'dialectical process', exploring how individuals move from basic sensory awareness to absolute knowledge.

Hegel's dialectical method involves understanding progress and change through contradictions.

It consists of:

1. Thesis: An existing state or idea.
2. Antithesis: Its contradiction or opposition.
3. Synthesis: The resolution that unites and transcends both.

For example, in the French Revolution, liberty (thesis) clashed with authoritarian rule (antithesis), leading to the modern constitutional state (synthesis). Some of the key concepts in phenomenology are:

1. Master-Slave Dialectic: This explains the development of self-awareness through relationships of dominance and dependence. For example, in colonialism, colonizers (masters) rely on the recognition of the colonized (slaves) for their identity, but the slaves, through struggle, assert independence, destabilizing the relationship.
2. Absolute Knowledge: This is the final stage of consciousness, where individuals and societies reconcile contradictions and recognize reality as a unified whole.

## Hegel's Influence on Thought

Hegel's dialectical method and exploration of consciousness had a profound impact on subsequent thinkers like:

- Karl Marx (1818–83), who adapted Hegelian dialectics to analyse class struggle, creating the framework of historical materialism.
- Jean-Paul Sartre (1905–80), who drew from Hegel's ideas on freedom and struggle in his existentialist exploration of human autonomy.
- Simone de Beauvoir (1908–86), who applied Hegel's master-slave dialectic to gender relations in *The Second Sex*.

## Challenging Traditional Beliefs

Hegel's philosophy questioned several prevailing intellectual paradigms of his time, including the Enlightenment's emphasis on reason, the mechanistic worldview of Newtonian physics and traditional dualistic interpretations of human existence. His ideas sought to reconcile contradictions and create a dynamic understanding of reality.

The Age of Enlightenment (seventeenth–eighteenth centuries) celebrated reason as the ultimate tool for understanding reality. Thinkers like René Descartes (1596–1650) introduced dualism, separating mind (res cogitans) and matter (res extensa) into distinct substances. Enlightenment thinkers like Immanuel Kant (1724–1804) stressed individual autonomy and rational inquiry as central to knowledge.

Hegel's Rejection of Dualism: Hegel argued that reality is a dynamic, unified whole, where mind and matter, subject and object, are interconnected and evolve together through contradictions. He saw Descartes's separation of mind and matter as overly simplistic.

For instance, instead of seeing a tree as merely physical (matter) or an idea in the mind (thought), Hegel underscored understanding the tree as part of a dynamic system, connecting human perception, nature and history.

Hegel's rejection of dualism influenced later thinkers like Martin Heidegger (1889–1976), who emphasized being-in-the-world, rejecting Descartes's division of humans from their environment; Maurice Merleau-Ponty (1908–61), who focused on the embodied nature of perception, underlining the unity of body and consciousness.

By challenging the Enlightenment's rationalist and mechanistic frameworks, Hegel opened the door to existentialist philosophy and phenomenology.

Hegel's Critique of Mechanistic Worldview: The Enlightenment also embraced the mechanistic worldview of Isaac Newton (1643–1727), who described the universe as a vast machine governed by fixed laws of motion and gravity. This deterministic view reduced nature to a predictable clockwork system. Hegel argued that reality is organic and dynamic, constantly evolving through contradictions.

Unlike Newton's predictable mechanics, human history unfolds unpredictably, driven by conflicts and resolutions. The French Revolution, for example, was not a mechanical inevitability but a result of deep contradictions between feudal privilege and emerging democratic ideals.

### Reinterpreting the Nature of Reality

Hegel introduced dialectics as a method to understand change. Instead of viewing opposites as incompatible, Hegel saw contradictions as the driving force of progress.

Freedom and authority seem contradictory, but their synthesis creates modern constitutional governance, balancing individual rights with collective responsibility. This dynamic view of reality influenced Karl Marx, who adapted dialectics to understand societal change through class struggle.

### Reinterpreting Christianity

Hegel's reinterpretation of Christianity was a revolutionary attempt to reconcile faith with philosophy, presenting religion as a dialectical process reflecting humanity's spiritual development.

During the Enlightenment, religion came under attack from rationalist philosophers like David Hume (1711–76), who criticized traditional doctrines as irrational. Hegel sought to defend Christianity, not as dogma but as a profound expression of humanity's spiritual evolution. Christianity had been reduced to a set of rigid beliefs. Hegel reimagined it as a living historical process, evolving alongside human consciousness.

Hegel interpreted the Christian doctrine of the Trinity as a metaphor for the development of self-consciousness and spirit.

1. Father (Unity): Represents the undifferentiated, absolute divine essence.
2. Son (Differentiation): Represents God's manifestation in the world, symbolizing the split between divine and human.
3. Holy Spirit (Reconciliation): Represents the unity of divine and human, achieved through community and shared understanding.

Hegel viewed Christianity as the highest stage in humanity's spiritual development, highlighting its historical evolution from ancient religions like Greek polytheism to Judaism, where the concept of a singular, transcendent God was introduced to Christianity as we know it, achieving the unity of the divine and human through the figure of Christ and the Holy Spirit.

Hegel's reinterpretation influenced modern theology, particularly the works of Paul Tillich (1886–1965), a theologian who argued that Christianity and philosophy share the same goal of uncovering ultimate truth and Karl Barth (1886–1968), a Protestant theologian who drew on Hegel's dialectics to explore the relationship between divine revelation and human history.

While Hegel's reinterpretation of Christianity was groundbreaking, it faced disapproval from existentialist thinkers like Søren Kierkegaard (1813–55). Kierkegaard believed Hegel's emphasis on the universal spirit overlooked the individual's personal relationship with God. Despite this, Hegel's ideas bridged the gap between faith and reason, influencing both religious and secular thought.

### Emergence of a New Worldview

Hegel's philosophy introduced a new worldview that underscored the dynamic, interconnected nature of reality. Rejecting the Enlightenment's static, mechanistic views of knowledge and society, he instead proposed that history, human consciousness and societal progress evolve through dialectical processes of contradictions and resolutions.

Historical Events as Dialectical Progress: Hegel viewed history as a rational process, where each stage represents a step towards the realization of freedom and self-consciousness. The French Revolution (1789–99) showcased the clash between freedom (thesis) and authority (antithesis), resulting in the emergence of modern constitutional governance (synthesis). Similarly, the abolition of slavery in the nineteenth century represented a resolution of humanity's struggle for universal dignity.

Influencing Marx, Sartre and Beauvoir: Marx adapted Hegel's dialectics to understand societal change through class struggle. While Hegel focused on ideas, Marx applied this method to material conditions. Marx's *Das Kapital* (1867) was built on Hegel's notion that contradictions drive historical progress, establishing the foundation of modern communism.

Sartre's existentialism, especially in *Being and Nothingness* (1943), was influenced by Hegel's exploration of struggle and recognition in human relationships. Sartre expanded on the master-slave dialectic to analyse how individuals assert freedom and shape their identities in oppressive systems.

In *The Second Sex* (1949), Beauvoir used Hegel's master-slave dialectic to probe gender dynamics. She argued that women have been defined as the 'Other' in relation to men, perpetuating social inequality. Beauvoir demonstrated how historical and cultural structures denied women recognition as full subjects.

**Absolute Idealism: Reality as Universal Spirit**

Hegel's absolute idealism posited that reality is a manifestation of a universal spirit (Geist), realized through history and human consciousness. The evolution of political systems from monarchy to democracy reflects the spirit's progress towards freedom. This worldview provided the foundation for diverse fields, from existentialism to political philosophy, stressing interconnectedness over fragmentation.

**Hegel's Contribution to Modern Political Philosophy**

Hegel played a seminal role in establishing political philosophy as a distinct field of intellectual inquiry. He combined insights from ethics, history and law to create a comprehensive framework for understanding the state, freedom and governance.

**1. The State as the Embodiment of Ethical Life**

He viewed the state as the highest expression of ethical life (Sittlichkeit), where individual freedom is realized within a rational, organized community.

A constitutional democracy balances individual rights with collective responsibilities, achieving ethical harmony.

**2. Freedom Through Rational Governance**

He argued that true freedom requires rational institutions that enable individuals to thrive.

Modern welfare states reconcile personal liberty with societal welfare, ensuring dignity for all citizens.

**3. Inspiring Future Political Thinkers**

His ideas shaped generations of political philosophers:

- Karl Marx (1818–83): Developed socialism and communism, critiquing capitalism's contradictions.
- John Rawls (1921–2002): In *A Theory of Justice* (1971), Rawls expanded on Hegel's ideas of fairness and equity in governance.

In *The Philosophy of Right*, Hegel argued that true freedom is not merely the ability to act without restriction. He challenged liberalism. He argued that individual rights must be balanced with the collective good. He was sceptical that political freedom could exist in a purely liberal society.

## ANECDOTES

### 1. Napoleon at Jena (1806)

Hegel witnessed Napoleon's entry into Jena, describing him as the 'world spirit on Horseback'. He saw Napoleon as embodying the rational progress of history, unifying Europe under modern political ideals.

This event reinforced Hegel's belief in history as a process driven by the realization of freedom.

### Why His Ideas Matter Today

Hegel's philosophy continues to shape contemporary thought, particularly in discussions on history, freedom and the role of the state. His dialectical method, where contradictions drive progress, has influenced fields ranging from political theory to social justice movements.

Marx's critique of capitalism drew heavily from Hegel's ideas while modern debates on governance, ethics and individual liberty still grapple with his central question: How can true freedom be achieved?

At the heart of Hegel's philosophy is the belief that freedom is not just about individual autonomy but about participation in ethical life, where individuals and institutions evolve through dialogue and conflict. This idea remains relevant in various fields:

1. Understanding Social Inequality: Hegel's dialectics offer a framework for analysing systemic injustices related to race, gender and class. His concept of recognition has influenced social movements and identity politics.
2. Freedom vs. Authority: His work informs debates on balancing personal liberties with collective responsibilities, a crucial issue in democratic governance.
3. Conflict Resolution: Hegel's method of resolving contradictions is widely applied in mediation, peace-building and political negotiations.
4. Bridging Disciplines: His ideas continue to unify fields like philosophy, theology and sociology, fostering interdisciplinary insights.
5. Influence on Feminism: Feminist theorists draw on Hegel's concepts of power and recognition to analyse gender dynamics and social structures.

By bridging faith and reason, individuality and community, Hegel's philosophy remains a powerful tool for understanding political systems, cultural transformations and personal struggles. His ideas continue to inspire thinkers across generations, reinforcing his place as a foundational figure in philosophy and political theory.

## JOHN STUART MILL: THE ADVOCATE FOR LIBERTY AND UTILITARIANISM

### Historical Context and Introduction

John Stuart Mill was born on 20 May 1806 in Pentonville, London, during a time of industrialization, expanding democracy and social change. The Industrial Revolution had turned Britain into a global powerhouse, bringing technological advancements but also social upheaval, poverty and widening economic inequality.

Politically, Britain was debating reforms to expand the franchise and address rising unrest among the working classes. The legacy of the French Revolution loomed large: It had championed liberty, equality and fraternity but had also triggered fears of chaos and instability.

Philosophically, the era was dominated by utilitarianism, led by Jeremy Bentham (1748–1832). Bentham's 'greatest happiness principle' proposed that laws and actions should be judged solely by their capacity to produce the greatest happiness for the greatest number. Mill's father, James Mill (1773–1836), a Scottish historian, economist and close associate of Bentham, worked at the East India Company. An ardent believer in Bentham's ideas, James Mill sought to create a genius who could advance utilitarian thought and contribute to societal reform.

This intellectual, political and economic environment deeply impacted John Stuart Mill's life and shaped his revolutionary ideas on liberty, equality and representative government.

## Brief Biography

John Stuart Mill's upbringing was an extraordinary experiment in education. James Mill, determined to raise a prodigy, imposed a rigourous and relentless curriculum. At the age of three, Mill began learning Greek, reading *Aesop's Fables* and Xenophon's *Anabasis*. By the age of eight, he had mastered Latin and was reading Plato's *Dialogues* and the works of Herodotus. At twelve, Mill was studying logic, advanced mathematics and political economy under his father's supervision, particularly the works of David Ricardo and Adam Smith.

Mill's intellectual growth came at the cost of emotional well-being. He was denied childhood friendships and leisure. In 1826, at the age of twenty, Mill suffered a mental crisis, feeling that his life and work lacked purpose. He felt like he had been turned into a 'thinking machine'. Reflecting on this period, he wrote, 'The whole foundation upon which my life was constructed fell down.'

His recovery began when he discovered William Wordsworth's poetry, which taught him the value of beauty, emotion and personal fulfilment. This period transformed Mill's philosophy, leading him to balance reason and logic with an appreciation for human happiness and individuality.

Over time, he became a key advocate for social reform, gender equality and political freedom. His most influential works include *On Liberty*, *Utilitarianism* and *The Subjection of Women*. His commitment to personal freedom, social justice and the well-being of society still influences modern liberal political thought.

## Core Contribution to Political Philosophy

Mill's intellectual development was deeply influenced by his father and the utilitarian philosopher Jeremy Bentham. Even though Mill inherited Benthamite utilitarianism, he transformed it into a more humane and nuanced philosophy.

Bentham's utilitarianism accentuated the quantity of happiness, often reducing morality to a mathematical calculation. Mill introduced qualitative distinctions, arguing that intellectual and moral pleasures were superior to physical ones. He famously said, 'It is better to be a human being dissatisfied than a pig satisfied.'

For example, reading a great work of literature, while requiring effort, offers deeper fulfilment than indulging in simple sensory pleasures.

His most famous works outlining his philosophical ideology include:

- *On Liberty* (1859): A seminal defense of individual liberty and free expression.
- *The Subjection of Women* (1869): A powerful critique of gender inequality and a call for equal rights.
- *Principles of Political Economy* (1848): A work combining classical economics with progressive ideas on poverty and labour.
- *Utilitarianism* (1863): A refined version of Bentham's philosophy that elevated human dignity and individuality.

### *On Liberty*: The Pathbreaking Concept of Democracy and Government

Mill is best known for his work on liberty and utilitarianism. In *On Liberty*, he argued that individual freedom is necessary for human development. He said that society should only limit individual liberty when it harms others. This idea, known as the 'harm principle', has been central to liberal political thought, especially in debates about personal freedom and the role of state.

Mill was inspired to write *On Liberty* through the observations of Victorian Britain, where majoritarian conformity was stifling individuality and dissent, state intervention in personal affairs was growing and the ideals of liberty introduced during the French Revolution were being ignored in practice.

Mill also drew from his own experiences. His emotional breakdown taught him the value of individuality and the need for a free, pluralistic society.

His core arguments were:

1. The Harm Principle: Individuals should be free to act as they please, provided their actions do not harm others.
   *Example:* Mill opposed laws banning alcohol unless drinking harmed others directly.
   *Relevance Today:* The harm principle underpins debates on euthanasia, drug decriminalization and digital privacy.
2. Freedom of Thought and Expression: Mill argued that even false opinions contribute to progress by challenging accepted truths. He said, 'The silencing of an opinion is robbing humanity.'
   *Example:* Galileo's scientific discoveries, once suppressed, later transformed our understanding of the universe.
   *Relevance Today:* Mill's defence of free speech remains central to debates on censorship, hate speech laws and social media regulation.
3. Tyranny of the Majority: Mill warned that democratic societies risk suppressing minority opinions through majority norms.
   *Example:* Victorian morality imposed conformity, silencing unconventional thinkers and reformers.

*Relevance Today:* Protecting minority rights, LGBTQ+ freedoms and religious pluralism reflects Mill's warning.

4. Individuality as a Component of Progress: Mill championed individuality as essential for personal and societal development.
   *Example:* Innovators, artists and reformers challenge norms and drive progress.
   *Relevance Today:* Diversity and inclusion policies foster creativity and societal resilience.

### Challenging Traditional Beliefs

J.S. Mill fearlessly confronted the entrenched norms of his time, offering transformative ideas that influenced modern society. Each of his challenges to tradition carried far-reaching impacts.

### Gender Inequality

Mill's book *The Subjection of Women* (1869) was revolutionary in advocating for equal rights for women. He argued that the subjugation of women was morally indefensible, economically detrimental and a hindrance to societal progress. He compared women's legal status to slavery, declaring that the subordination of half the population was incompatible with a just society. He famously said, 'The legal subordination of one sex to the other is wrong in itself and now one of the chief hindrances to human improvement.'

Mill's ideas were initially met with ridicule and resistance. In Parliament, many viewed women's equality as unnatural and unthinkable. However, it was a great influence on the Women's Suffrage Movement. Mill became the first MP to introduce a motion for women's suffrage in 1867, which although defeated, galvanized the suffragette movement in Britain.

In the present world, Mill's arguments have been pivotal in laying the foundation for laws promoting gender equality, including equal pay legislation and women's property rights. His ideas continue to inspire debates on closing gender gaps in leadership and education.

## Censorship and Freedom of Expression

Mill argued in *On Liberty* that freedom of thought and expression were vital to human progress. Silencing dissent, he maintained, deprives society of truth as even erroneous ideas challenge prevailing beliefs and strengthen understanding. He cited Galileo's persecution for proposing heliocentrism, which was initially condemned but later recognized as scientific truth.

Victorian society, dominated by rigid moral codes, often viewed dissent and unconventional opinions as dangerous. Mill's ideas were radical for their time. However, in today's world, Mill's principles underpin free speech laws and inform debates on censorship and hate speech regulation in the digital age. The 'marketplace of ideas' concept remains vital in legal and political discourse.

## Child Labour and Education

Mill criticized the exploitation of children in factories, advocating for laws to protect their welfare and ensure access to education. He believed education was the cornerstone of a free, informed and responsible citizenry.

*In Principles of Political Economy*, Mill argued that the state must intervene to secure education for all children as ignorance perpetuates inequality. His call for child labour laws was resisted by industrialists, claiming they would disrupt economic growth.

Mill's advocacy influenced the establishment of compulsory education laws and continues to guide policies combating child labour and promoting universal education.

### Economic Inequality and Labour Rights

Unlike Bentham, Mill recognized that unchecked capitalism deepened inequality. He supported progressive policies to redistribute wealth, ensure fair labour conditions, and uplift the working class.

He proposed progressive taxation, arguing that the wealthy had a moral duty to contribute more to society. He also supported cooperative ownership, where workers would share profits and ownership of enterprises.

His ideas were considered radical as Victorian society largely accepted the laissez-faire economic model. Later, it influenced the creation of welfare states, progressive taxation policies and debates on income inequality and workers' rights in the twenty-first century.

### Religious Dogma and Secular Governance

Mill opposed the dominance of religious orthodoxy in public life, advocating for secular governance, where no single religion could dictate state policy or limit individual freedoms. He argued against blasphemy laws and defended the right of individuals to question religious authority without fear of persecution.

For this, he faced opposition from religious leaders, who viewed his ideas as threats to societal morality. His principles remain central to secular democracies, informing debates on religious freedom, the separation of church and state and blasphemy laws.

**Colonial Exploitation**

While Mill worked for the East India Company, he became increasingly critical of colonial oppression. He argued for self-determination and more humane governance in colonies. In his writings on India, Mill acknowledged the need to educate and empower colonized populations, though his views remained complex and sometimes contradictory.

British colonial administrators largely ignored Mill's calls for reform during his time. But his arguments for self-governance inspired postcolonial movements and remain relevant in debates on human rights and international justice.

**Marriage and Family**

Mill's views on marriage were radical for his time. He argued that marriage should be a partnership of equals, free from patriarchal dominance.

Mill's relationship with Harriet Taylor Mill reflected these ideals. Harriet, a writer and intellectual, co-developed Mill's ideas on liberty and gender equality. Mill described her as his 'intellectual equal and inspiration'.

Even though Victorian society dismissed Mill's views as subversive to family values, they have influenced movements for women's reproductive rights and legal frameworks ensuring equality within marriage.

## ANECDOTES

### 1. The Child Prodigy and Plato

John Stuart Mill's prodigious childhood is a striking example of his father's experiment in education. At the age of eight, Mill had mastered Latin and was immersed in Plato's *Republic*, a text examining justice and the ideal state. James Mill would often engage young Mill in debates over Plato's ideas, treating him as an intellectual peer.

This early exposure to Greek philosophy laid the foundation for Mill's deep engagement with political philosophy and his focus on liberty and justice. However, it also reflects the pressure Mill faced as a child, which later contributed to his mental breakdown. It demonstrates the duality of his upbringing – intellectual brilliance nurtured at the cost of emotional development.

### 2. Harriet Taylor Mill: The Intellectual Partner

Mill's relationship with Harriet Taylor, whom he eventually married in 1851, was one of deep intellectual and emotional companionship. Harriet, an accomplished thinker and writer, profoundly shaped Mill's work on gender equality, liberty and justice. They collaborated on several works, including *The Subjection of Women*.

Harriet's sharp insights and critiques pushed Mill to refine his arguments and to boldly articulate his feminist ideals. Mill later wrote about her, 'To her intellect, its cultivation, and its activity, I owe much.'

At a time when women were excluded from public discourse, Mill's partnership with Harriet was groundbreaking.

Their relationship embodied the ideals of equality and respect that Mill advocated for in *The Subjection of Women*. It also highlights Harriet's role as an unsung contributor to modern liberal thought.

**4. Defending Women's Rights in Parliament (1867)**

In 1867, during Mill's time as a Member of Parliament, he proposed an amendment to the Second Reform Act to include women's suffrage. When met with ridicule and claims that his proposal was 'unnatural' and 'un-English', Mill stood his ground with a sharp retort, 'To deny political rights to half the human race on the ground of sex alone is arbitrary and unjust.' Though the amendment was defeated, Mill's advocacy for women's suffrage made him a pioneer of the movement and inspired future activists like Millicent Fawcett.

This illustrates Mill's courage in challenging societal norms. Despite resistance, he championed gender equality as a moral and political necessity, laying the intellectual foundation for the eventual success of the women's suffrage movement.

**Why His Ideas Matter Today**

John Stuart Mill's ideas remain foundational to addressing contemporary challenges. His work on liberty, democracy and equality continues to influence political and social discourse today.

Mill's defence of freedom of expression underpins legal debates on digital censorship, social media regulation and academic freedom. His 'harm principle is frequently cited in discussions about the limits of speech and the role of government in regulating content. His arguments for women's rights inspire movements advocating for equal pay, political representation and reproductive freedoms. His work *The Subjection of Women* remains a cornerstone for feminist philosophy and gender equality advocacy. Mill's analysis of inequality has been influential in policies on progressive taxation, workers' rights and universal education. His views on economic distribution and social justice continue to shape modern discussions on wealth disparity and labour rights. Mill's call for secular governance remains vital in diverse multicultural societies. His stress on religious tolerance informs contemporary debates on the separation of church and state.

**Contribution to Political Philosophy**

Mill made political philosophy a distinct and rigourous discipline by bridging ethical theory with practical governance. His contributions laid the base for modern liberal democracies.

- Representative Government: In *Considerations on Representative Government*, Mill advocated for democracy while warning against the 'tyranny of the majority'. He supported proportional representation to ensure minority voices were heard, a principle still debated in electoral reform movements today.
- Individual Liberty: Mill placed individual autonomy at the heart of political systems, arguing that liberty drives progress and innovation. His work continues to influence discussions on personal freedoms and government intervention.
- Active Citizenship: He believed democracy required an educated and engaged electorate. He championed

the idea that citizens must actively participate in governance to ensure a just and functional democracy.

Mill's ideas influenced the development of modern constitutional democracies, inspiring protections for civil liberties and minority rights. His advocacy for proportional representation is still relevant in electoral reforms worldwide while his principles on liberty and self-development still shape discussions on individual rights, democracy and social justice.

John Stuart Mill was a towering intellectual whose work transformed political philosophy, ethics and society's understanding of liberty. By challenging tradition and offering nuanced ideas on freedom, equality and representative government, he laid the foundation for modern liberal democracies. His principles continue to inspire efforts for justice, human dignity and social progress, reminding us that a free, educated and equal society is the key to enduring progress.

## KARL MARX: THE REVOLUTIONARY THINKER OF CLASS STRUGGLE AND COMMUNISM

### Historical Context and Introduction

Karl Marx was born on 5 May 1818 in Trier, in the Kingdom of Prussia, now modern-day Germany. This era was marked by the Industrial Revolution, a transformative period that reshaped economies and societies across Europe. Steam-powered machinery and mechanized production drove rapid industrialization, creating unprecedented wealth for industrialists while deepening economic inequality.

The bourgeoisie, or capitalist class, controlled the means of production, while the proletariat, or working class, laboured under harsh conditions for meagre wages. Movements like the Chartist protests in England (1838–57), which demanded political and social reforms, reflected rising discontent among workers. The Revolutions of 1848, across Europe, further highlighted the growing divide between social classes.

This turbulent backdrop and growing disparity fuelled Marx's revolutionary critique of capitalism. His ideas helped mould socialist and communist movements and revolutionized political philosophy, economics and the study of class relations.

**Brief Biography**

Karl Marx was born into a middle-class family. His father, Heinrich Marx, was a lawyer inspired by Enlightenment ideals like reason, liberty and progress. Heinrich encouraged. Karl to question authority, a trait that would define his intellectual and revolutionary pursuits.

At the University of Bonn and later the University of Berlin, Marx initially studied law but soon gravitated towards philosophy and history. It was in Berlin that he encountered the works of Georg Wilhelm Friedrich Hegel (1770–1831). Hegel's dialectical framework, which posited that progress arises through contradictions, had a deep impact on Marx. However, Marx adapted Hegel's method, focusing on material conditions rather than abstract ideas, which became the foundation of his own historical materialism.

During this time, Marx became associated with the Young Hegelians, a group of radical thinkers critiquing religion, politics and societal norms. This association sparked Marx's early criticisms of organized religion and state authority, setting the stage for his later revolutionary theories on class, economics and power.

Marx's intellectual journey began with his studies in law and philosophy, but his major contributions came through his partnership with Friedrich Engels. Together, they co-authored several influential works, including *The Communist Manifesto* and *Das Kapital*. Marx spent much of his life in exile in London, where he continued his research and writing. Despite personal hardships and political opposition, his ideas laid the groundwork for political movements that would later shape much of the twentieth century, including the Russian Revolution and the rise of Marxist–Leninist governments.

## Core Contribution to Political Philosophy

Marx's intellectual framework was modelled by a synthesis of ideas from key thinkers like Adam Smith (1723–90) and David Ricardo (1772–1823), the classical economists whose labour theories of value Marx expanded into his concept of surplus value. French utopian socialists like Claude Henri de Rouvroy, Comte de Saint-Simon (1760–1825) and Charles Fourier (1772–1837) formed Marx's radical ideas on societal transformation. He also adopted Hegel's dialectical method but directed it on material realities rather than abstract ideas.

Marx's most significant contribution is his theory of historical materialism, which suggests that the structure of society depends on its economic base – the way goods are produced and distributed. He argues that the economic base of society determines its superstructure, including culture, politics and religion. For example, the transition from feudalism to capitalism was driven not by ideological change but by shifts in production and trade.

According to Marx, history is defined by class struggles, where each economic system (feudalism, capitalism, socialism) involves a conflict between the ruling class (owners of the means of production) and the working class (those who sell their labour). This materialist perspective provided a new lens for understanding historical development and societal change.

### *The Communist Manifesto*: A Revolutionary Call to Action

*The Communist Manifesto* (1848), co-written by Karl Marx and Friedrich Engels, remains one of the most influential political documents in history. Published at the request of the Communist League during the revolutionary upheavals of 1848, the manifesto offered a concise critique of capitalism and a bold vision for a socialist future.

- **Historical Materialism and Class Struggle:** Marx and Engels proposed that history is defined by class struggles, from the feudal lords versus serfs of the Middle Ages to the bourgeoisie versus proletariat under capitalism. They argued that capitalism's internal contradictions would inevitably lead to its downfall, just as feudalism had been replaced by capitalism. For example, Marx used the transition from agrarian economies to industrialized societies to demonstrate how material changes in production lead to shifts in social and political systems. The bourgeoisie, who once spearheaded revolutionary change, now embodied the exploitative ruling class.

- **The Proletariat's Exploitation:** The manifesto described capitalism as inherently exploitative. The bourgeoisie extracted surplus value from the proletariat's labour while paying them subsistence wages. For instance, factory workers who toiled fourteen-hour days in the textile industries of nineteenth-century Britain earned meager wages, enriching the capitalists disproportionately.
- **Revolutionary Praxis and the Role of Communists:** Unlike utopian socialists, Marx and Engels argued for the necessity of organized, collective action to dismantle capitalist structures. Their rallying cry, 'Workers of the world, unite!' lay emphasis on solidarity across national borders and industries. They envisioned a proletarian revolution that would establish socialism as a transitional phase towards a classless, stateless communist society.
- **Global Perspective and Prediction:** Marx and Engels were remarkably prescient in predicting globalization's role in capitalism's expansion. They noted how capitalism transcends borders, turning local economies into components of a global market while simultaneously sowing the seeds of its own destruction through growing inequalities and crises.

The manifesto's vision of economic justice and equality inspired revolutionary movements, from Russia's Bolsheviks to the Chinese Communist Party. It remains a foundational text for labour unions, social movements and political parties advocating for systemic change.

## *Das Kapital:* A Systematic Critique of Capitalism

While *The Communist Manifesto* laid out a revolutionary framework, *Das Kapital* (Volume I, 1867) was Marx's magnum opus, offering a comprehensive analysis of capitalism's economic mechanisms and systemic contradictions. Unlike polemical works, *Das Kapital* used empirical data and rigourous argumentation to review capitalist economies.

### 1. Commodity Fetishism

Marx argued that commodities obscure the social relationships underlying their production. For instance, a mass-produced smartphone is valued for its utility and market price, hiding the exploitative labour conditions in factories. This 'fetishism' turns relationships between people into relationships between objects, dehumanizing labour.

### 2. Surplus Value and Exploitation

Surplus value, a cornerstone of Marx's critique, represents the difference between the value created by labour and the wages paid to workers. For example, a worker might produce 10,000 worth of goods in a day but earn only 2,000; the remaining 8,000 becomes the capitalist's profit. This dynamic perpetuates inequality by concentrating wealth in the hands of a few.

### 3. Accumulation and Crisis

Marx identified capitalism's cyclical crises as intrinsic to the system. Overproduction leads to economic stagnation, lay-offs and recessions. Examples include the 1929 Great Depression and the 2008 financial crisis, which exposed capitalism's vulnerabilities.

### 4. Labour and Alienation

Marx expanded on alienation, pointing out how workers are estranged from the products of their labour, their fellow workers and their humanity. Factory labourers producing identical goods on assembly lines exemplify this alienation, with little control over the creative process or the end product.

*Das Kapital* remains a seminal text for understanding economic inequality, critiquing globalization and analysing systemic crises. It informs debates on issues ranging from labour rights to environmental sustainability.

### Marxism vs. Communism

Marxism refers to the theoretical framework developed by Karl Marx and Friedrich Engels. It encompasses historical materialism, dialectical materialism and critiques of political economy. It seeks to analyse and change society by addressing the material and economic conditions that shape social relations.

Communism, as envisioned by Marx, represents the final stage of societal evolution – a stateless, classless society where the means of production are communally owned. This contrasts sharply with state-led regimes that have historically appropriated the label 'communist'.

While Marxism provides a theoretical framework, communism often refers to the practical implementation of these ideas, which has varied widely. Although Marx envisioned communism as stateless, communist regimes like the USSR and China retained centralized state control. However, Marxism and communism both aim to abolish class divisions and create a society based on equality, collective ownership and social justice.

## Women, Domestic Labour and Marxism

Marx's analysis of class and production has been extended by Marxist feminists to examine the intersection of capitalism and gender oppression.

Capitalism relies on unpaid domestic labour, predominantly performed by women, to sustain the workforce, predominantly men. This labour – childcare, cooking, cleaning – is essential yet excluded from formal economic systems. By framing domestic labour as a private, gendered responsibility, capitalism perpetuates systemic inequality.

For instance, in industrialized societies, women often face a 'double burden', balancing paid employment with unpaid domestic responsibilities. Policies such as subsidized childcare and paid parental leave have roots in Marxist critiques of economic inequality.

In *The Origin of the Family, Private Property, and the State* (1884), Engels linked women's subjugation to the rise of private property. He argued that patriarchal family structures emerged to ensure the inheritance of property through male lineage, reinforcing gender and class oppression.

Modern movements advocating for equal pay, reproductive rights and the recognition of care work often draw from Marxist feminist analyses. The gig economy further highlights these issues, with women disproportionately represented in low-paying, precarious jobs.

Marxist feminism extends Marxist theory to analyse how capitalism perpetuates gender inequality. It highlights the interconnectedness of class oppression and patriarchy, arguing that economic systems exploit women's labour in both the domestic and public spheres.

## Core Ideas of Marxist Feminism

- **Reproductive Labour:** Marxist feminists argue that capitalism relies on unpaid reproductive labour – childbearing, caregiving and household work – to sustain the labour force. This work, often performed by women, is essential yet unacknowledged in economic systems. For example, childcare enables workers to participate in the economy, but its value is not reflected in GDP or wages.
- **The Double Burden:** Women in capitalist societies often face a double burden, balancing paid employment with unpaid domestic responsibilities. This dual exploitation reinforces systemic inequalities, as seen in industries like garment manufacturing, where women are overrepresented in low-paying, risky jobs.
- **Capitalism's Reinforcement of Gender Roles:** Capitalist systems perpetuate traditional gender roles, confining women to 'natural' roles as caregivers while assigning men the role of breadwinners. This dynamic marginalizes women in both the workplace and the political sphere.

## Exponents of Marxist Feminism

Marxist feminism has been shaped by powerful thinkers who have analysed the intersection of gender and class struggle, the role of women in revolutionary movements and critiquing capitalist systems for perpetuating gender oppression.

Clara Zetkin, a prominent Marxist feminist, championed the rights of working-class women and played a crucial role in organizing the first International Women's Day in 1911, advocating for suffrage, labour rights and social reforms.

Alexandra Kollontai, a key figure in the Bolshevik movement, worked to integrate gender equality into socialist policies and became the first female government minister in Soviet history. She advanced progressive policies like maternity leave, childcare facilities and equal pay.

More recently, Silvia Federici, in her seminal work *Caliban and the Witch* (2004), examined how the rise of capitalism reinforced gender oppression. She argued that the witch hunts of early modern Europe were a means to control women's bodies and labour, setting the stage for capitalist exploitation.

These thinkers have contributed significantly to the understanding of how patriarchy and capitalism overlap, shaping the discourse on gender and economic justice. Marxist feminism has been instrumental in advocating for the recognition of domestic labour as productive work. Addressing wage disparities and championing workplace rights, particularly for women in low-wage sectors. Challenging traditional gender roles, fostering greater participation of women in political and economic decision-making.

### Contribution to Political Philosophy

Marx's contributions to political philosophy reformed debates on power, legitimacy and the state. He argued that the state is not a neutral entity but a tool for maintaining the dominance of the ruling class. For example, laws protecting private property primarily benefit the bourgeoisie, reinforcing systemic inequality.

Marx's activism complemented his theoretical work. As a leader of the First International (International Workingmen's Association), he sought to unite workers' movements globally, highlighting the importance of international solidarity. Marx's vision of a stateless, classless society continues to influence debates on governance, justice and revolution.

## ANECDOTES

### 1. Financial Struggles and *Das Kapital*

Marx lived in extreme poverty for much of his life, often pawning his belongings to provide for his family while working on *Das Kapital*. His London residence was marked by unpaid debts, illness and the tragic loss of several of his children due to poor living conditions.

These hardships were not just personal – they embodied the very capitalist inequalities he criticized. Marx's financial struggles reinforced his belief in class struggle, exploitation and the urgent need for proletarian revolution.

### 2. Exile and Revolutionary Activism

Forced out of Germany, France and Belgium for his radical views, Marx eventually found refuge in London in 1849. Despite living in exile, he remained deeply involved in European revolutionary movements, corresponding with activists and shaping socialist thought across the continent.

His displacement gave him a global perspective on capitalism as he observed industrialization and class struggles in different nations. Exile also influenced his concept of international proletarian solidarity, which became central to his *Communist Manifesto.*

### 3. The Helene Demuth Affair: A Personal Contradiction

Marx's household included Helene Demuth, a domestic worker who had been with his family since his youth. In a private scandal, Marx fathered an illegitimate child with her, a stark contradiction to his advocacy for gender and class equality.

To avoid public disgrace, Friedrich Engels falsely claimed paternity of the child. This reveals the complexities of Marx's personal life, raising questions about the intersection of his ideals and actions.

### Why His Ideas Matter Today

Karl Marx remains a towering figure in modern thought, whose critique of capitalism continues to shape discussions on inequality, labour and societal transformation. His theories provide a framework for understanding key socio-economic challenges:

- Economic Inequality: The growing wealth gap aligns with Marx's prediction that capitalism concentrates wealth in the hands of a few. The rise of multinational corporations and corporate power further highlights class divisions.
- Labour Exploitation: Precarious employment, the gig economy and global supply chains mirror Marx's criticism of surplus value extraction and worker alienation.
- Technological Disruption: Automation and AI challenge traditional labour structures, raising questions about employment and economic security.
- Environmental Crises: Capitalism's focus on profit over sustainability contributes to environmental degradation, a contradiction Marx's framework helps explain.
- Political Influence: While the fall of the Soviet Union (1991) exposed the failures of state-led Marxist regimes,

Marx's vision of a classless society continues to inspire movements for justice and equality.

From *The Communist Manifesto* to *Das Kapital,* Marx's works remain indispensable for critiquing inequality and imagining a more equitable world. Though the practical application of Marxism has been controversial, his insights remain vital in analysing modern global challenges.

## MAX WEBER: THE SOCIOLOGIST WHO BRIDGED PHILOSOPHY AND POLITICAL THEORY

### Historical Context and Introduction

Max Weber, born on 21 April 1864 in Erfurt, Prussia, came of age during a transformative period in European history. The unification of Germany in 1871, under Otto von Bismarck, marked a monumental shift in European geopolitics, fostering a national identity that Weber later dissected in his theories on authority and legitimacy. The rapid industrialization of Germany, propelling it into the forefront of European economic power, exposed Weber to the tensions between traditional structures and emerging capitalist systems. This dual exposure to political consolidation and economic upheaval influenced his exploration of modernity, rationalization and the disenchantment of the world.

The rise of the nation-state also framed Weber's thoughts on political authority. He witnessed the Prussian bureaucracy, a model of efficiency, control and rational governance, expand its influence during this time, serving as a foundation for his studies on legal-rational authority.

The Prussian bureaucracy was one of the most developed administrative systems in nineteenth-century Europe, known for its structured hierarchy, merit-based appointments and efficiency. Established during the reign of Frederick the Great, it played a key role in transforming Prussia into a modern state. Bureaucrats were expected to give precedence to duty over personal interests, personifying the ideals of discipline and rational governance. However, Weber's observations of this system revealed its dual nature: While it ensured administrative efficiency, it also highlighted the dehumanizing effects of rigid rules and impersonal structures.

Weber was particularly critical of how such bureaucratic systems, despite their benefits, could create what he termed the 'iron cage'. He argued that the mechanistic nature of bureaucracy often undermined individual autonomy and creativity. For Weber, the Prussian model epitomized this paradox: a structure designed to serve society yet capable of alienating individuals through excessive rationalization.

His work had a great impact on both sociology and political philosophy. A contemporary of figures like Karl Marx and Friedrich Nietzsche, Weber's work emerged during the shift from traditional to modern societies, which challenged conventional ways of thinking about politics, authority and social structures.

His reflections on bureaucracy, the nature of authority and the role of religion in social life are key contributions that continue to impact both social sciences and political thought. His work delved into the complexities of political power, how authority gains legitimacy and how institutions impact individual freedom.

## Brief Biography

Weber's upbringing in an intellectually vibrant household was instrumental in shaping his future work. His father, Max Weber Sr., a politician and lawyer, often hosted political debates at home, exposing young Weber to contemporary issues of governance and policy. These discussions, however, were often contentious, causing conflicts between his father's authoritarian tendencies and his mother Helene's deeply moral and religious values. This domestic dynamic introduced Weber to the complexities of authority and morality, themes he later explored in his studies of power and legitimacy.

As a student, Weber's experiences reflected the shifting intellectual landscape of nineteenth-century Germany. At the University of Heidelberg, his initial focus on law soon expanded to include history, economics and philosophy, areas that would later define his multidisciplinary approach. His formative years were marked by rigourous engagement with the works of Immanuel Kant, G.W.F. Hegel and Friedrich Nietzsche, whose ideas on morality, rationality and individualism deeply influenced Weber's intellectual trajectory.

Weber's academic journey took him through some of the most prestigious universities in Germany, including Heidelberg, Berlin and Göttingen. These institutions exposed him to a diverse array of intellectual traditions and rigourous academic environments.

At Heidelberg, Weber immersed himself in debates on the intersection of law and economics, often engaging professors in spirited discussions. Weber even challenged his economics professor's deterministic views on industrial development, arguing instead for the role of cultural factors – a perspective that would later define his work on capitalism.

During his time at the University of Berlin, Weber frequented the city's intellectual salons, where he interacted with leading thinkers of the time. These gatherings provided a fertile ground for his ideas, particularly his interest in the sociology of religion. His exposure to wide-ranging disciplines and debates at these universities reinforced his belief in an interdisciplinary approach, evident in his groundbreaking analyses of religion, economics and politics.

He went on to teach at various German universities, including Heidelberg, and played a key role in the development of sociology as a discipline. Despite his academic success, Weber struggled with health issues and had to often step away from academia.

His intellectual career spanned multiple fields, including law, economics, history and sociology. His interdisciplinary approach to social theory made him one of the most influential social scientists. He was also active in political and intellectual debates, providing a critical, yet nuanced perspective on modern politics. Weber died in 1920 at the age of fifty-six, but his ideas continue to shape our understanding of authority, politics and society.

### Core Contribution to Political Philosophy

Max Weber's work in political philosophy reshaped the understanding of power, authority and the interplay between culture and society. His exploration of the nature of authority, the rise of bureaucracy and the influence of religion on social behaviour have left an indelible mark on political thought. Through his nuanced analysis of these phenomena, Weber provided a framework for understanding the forces that govern modern society. His ideas continue to influence political theory, sociology and the study of governance, offering deep insights into the challenges and complexities of the contemporary world.

## Core of Verstehen

Weber's concept of 'Verstehen' (interpretive understanding) was a methodological innovation that set him apart from other sociologists of his time. Verstehen emphasizes understanding social actions from the perspective of the actor, focusing on the subjective meanings individuals assign to their behaviour. Unlike positivist approaches, which sought to explain human behaviour solely through observable phenomena, Weber's Verstehen aimed to uncover the underlying motivations and intentions that drive actions.

Weber was inspired by Wilhelm Dilthey's ideas on the distinction between natural and social sciences. Dilthey argued that while natural sciences explain phenomena through causality, social sciences require an empathetic understanding of human experiences. Building on this foundation, Weber integrated Verstehen into his sociological method, elevating it as a tool for interpreting the complex interplay of culture, ideas and individual agency.

This approach stood out in contrast to the deterministic frameworks of Marx and Durkheim. For instance, while Marx stressed on economic structures in shaping society, Weber used Verstehen to explore how religious beliefs, such as Calvinist doctrines, influenced economic behaviour, as seen in *The Protestant Ethic and the Spirit of Capitalism*. Similarly, Weber's analysis of charismatic authority relied on Verstehen to grasp the personal appeal of leaders like Napoleon or Bismarck, rather than reducing their influence to institutional factors.

### Impact of Religion, Bureaucracy, Legitimacy and Globalization

Weber's contributions have had a lasting impact across multiple disciplines, reshaping the way we understand society, economics and politics. His ideas remain foundational in sociology, political science and organizational studies.

**Sociology of Religion:** Weber's exploration of religion as a force shaping economic and social behaviour has been instrumental in understanding cultural differences. His comparative studies of Protestantism, Hinduism and Confucianism revealed how religious values influenced economic systems. For example, his work showed why capitalism thrived in the West but not in India or China, where religious traditions emphasized otherworldly pursuits over material success.

**Bureaucracy and Rationalization:** Weber's critique of bureaucracy as a rational yet dehumanizing system remains highly relevant. Modern corporations, with their rigid hierarchies and performance metrics, exemplify the iron cage Weber warned about. His insights are frequently cited in organizational studies, where scholars evaluate the trade-offs between efficiency and employee well-being.

**Authority and Legitimacy:** Weber's classification of authority into traditional, charismatic and legal-rational types has deeply impacted political science. This framework helps explain phenomena ranging from the rise of authoritarian regimes to the stability of democratic institutions. For instance, Weber's theory sheds light on how leaders like Hitler rose to power by leveraging charismatic authority, transitioning it into institutional control.

**Globalization and Secularization:** Weber's ideas on rationalization and disenchantment offer a lens to understand contemporary challenges, such as the global spread of secularism and the increasing dominance of technocratic governance. His work on the Protestant ethic continues to inform debates on the cultural roots of economic disparities, particularly in the context of globalization.

## The Protestant Ethic and the Spirit of Capitalism

Weber's seminal work, *The Protestant Ethic and the Spirit of Capitalism*, examines the cultural roots of modern capitalism. Written during a period of rapid industrialization and secularization in Europe, the book explores how religious values shaped economic behaviour and challenged materialist interpretations of history.

Weber identified Calvinist doctrines, particularly predestination and the concept of a 'calling', as fostering a disciplined, frugal lifestyle that aligned with capitalist values. This ascetic ethos redirected wealth accumulation into productive investments, creating an economic environment conducive to capitalist growth. Weber's concept of the iron cage critiques the unintended consequences of rationalization, where individuals become trapped in systems prioritizing efficiency over humanity. His analysis remains a foundational text in understanding the cultural dimensions of economic systems.

### Weber and Marx: Contrasts and Parallels

Marx and Weber, though both towering intellectual figures, approached the study of society from fundamentally different angles. This discussion is crucial because their contrasting views illuminate the broader debates about the forces shaping modernity.

Marx emphasized economic structures, viewing class struggles as the primary drivers of historical change. In contrast, Weber highlighted the role of ideas, culture and institutions. For instance, Weber's thesis on Protestant ethics as a catalyst for capitalism challenges

Marx's materialist perspective that capitalism emerged solely from changes in the modes of production.

However, the two thinkers shared concerns about the alienation of individuals in modern systems. Marx criticized the exploitative nature of capitalism, while Weber focused on the dehumanizing effects of bureaucracy and rationalization. Together, their ideas offer complementary insights into the complexities of modernity.

### *Economy and Society*

Max Weber's most significant contributions to political philosophy focus on authority, power and the role of bureaucracy. In his classic work *Economy and Society*, he identified three types of authority:

1. Traditional authority: Based on long-standing customs and traditions.

2. Charismatic authority: Based on an individual's qualities and leadership.
3. Legal-rational authority: Based on established laws, rules and modern bureaucratic systems.

Weber argued that modern societies increasingly rely on legal-rational authority, particularly through bureaucracies. While he saw bureaucracy as efficient, he also warned of their potential to stifle individual freedom and create an iron cage of rationalization. This metaphor refers to how rigid bureaucratic systems can suppress creativity and reduce people to mere cogs in a large machine.

Weber also introduced 'value-free sociology', urging social scientists to study society objectively, without personal biases or political agendas. Though debated, it has had a lasting impact on the field of social research.

## ANECDOTES

### 1. The Nervous Breakdown

In the 1890s, Weber suffered a severe nervous breakdown, forcing him to withdraw from academia for several years. Plagued by insomnia and depression, he struggled with the very pressures of modernity that he later theorized.

During this period of self-reflection, Weber deepened his exploration of disenchantment, rationalization and bureaucracy. His personal struggles gave his theories an added depth, as he intimately understood the psychological cost of an increasingly rationalized world.

### 2. The Fearless Critic of Orthodoxy

Weber was known for his sharp intellect and fearless criticisms of established ideas. During heated academic debates, he often clashed with scholars who adhered to deterministic economic theories, insisting that cultural and religious values played a crucial role in determining social systems.

His ability to challenge prevailing theories, particularly Marxist materialism, earned him both admiration and apprehension among his peers. Weber's insistence on multidimensional analysis laid the base for his groundbreaking work on the Protestant ethic and capitalism.

### 3. Intellectual Partnership with Marianne Weber

Weber's wife, Marianne Weber, was a distinguished intellectual and feminist thinker in her own right. Their relationship was marked by mutual respect and scholarly collaboration. She supported Weber during his health crises and played a crucial role in preserving and publishing his works after his death.

Marianne's contributions ensured Weber's intellectual legacy while her own feminist writings reflected the broader sociological themes that he explored, particularly in relation to gender and social structures.

## Why His Ideas Matter Today

Max Weber's insights remain essential for understanding modern institutions, power structures and cultural dynamics. His analysis of bureaucracy is particularly relevant in today's world, where governments, corporations and other organizations are shaped by rigid bureaucratic systems. His warning about the iron cage of rationalization resonates in an era where efficiency and specialization often come at the cost of human values, autonomy and creativity.

Weber's theories on authority provide a crucial framework for investigating contemporary politics. In an age of rising populism and charismatic leadership, his work explains how different forms of authority shape legitimacy and governance. His exploration of religion's influence on capitalism also continues to inform discussions on how cultural and ideological forces affect global economic and political systems.

Beyond these specific applications, Weber's emphasis on historical and cultural context remains foundational in social science. His advocacy for objective, empirical research laid the groundwork for modern sociology, even as debates continue over the possibility of truly value-free inquiry.

Weber's intellectual legacy endures as a cornerstone for studying modernity. His critiques of bureaucracy, authority and cultural influence on economic behaviour remain relevant in debates about institutional overreach, surveillance capitalism and global economic disparities. By weaving history, sociology and political theory into a cohesive narrative, Weber offers timeless insights into the interplay of ideas, institutions and individual agency, providing valuable lessons for navigating today's complex world.

## FRIEDRICH NIETZSCHE: THE PHILOSOPHER OF INDIVIDUALISM AND THE WILL TO POWER

### Historical Context and Introduction

Friedrich Nietzsche was born on 15 October 1844 in Röcken, a small village in the Prussian Province of Saxony, Germany.

His lifetime coincided with one of the most turbulent and transformative periods in European history. The Revolutions of 1848, fuelled by demands for democracy and workers' rights, swept across the continent but failed to achieve lasting change, leaving behind a sense of disillusionment. Simultaneously, the unification of Germany in 1871 under Otto von Bismarck signalled the rise of nationalism and militarism, shaping the political and cultural atmosphere of Nietzsche's adult years.

The Industrial Revolution brought unprecedented technological and scientific advancements, but it also disrupted traditional ways of life. Urbanization, mechanization and the growing influence of materialism created new social tensions. Religion, long a cornerstone of European identity, faced challenges from Darwinian evolution, Enlightenment rationalism and burgeoning secularism. Nietzsche's philosophy emerged as a response to this cultural vacuum, critiquing the inadequacy of traditional values to address the existential dilemmas of modernity.

The tension of this era intensely affected Nietzsche's thought. He lived through a time when old certainties were crumbling but new frameworks had yet to emerge. This statement encapsulated the spiritual disorientation of a world transitioning from religious faith to secular modernity. His work had a lasting impact on existentialism and postmodern philosophy.

### Brief Biography

Nietzsche's childhood was marked by both privilege and tragedy. His father, Carl Ludwig Nietzsche, a Lutheran pastor, died from a brain ailment when Friedrich was only five years old, leaving his deeply religious mother, Franziska, to raise him and his younger sister, Elisabeth, in a household dominated by Christian piety. Röcken, his birthplace, was a rural and insular community, steeped in Lutheran traditions, which Nietzsche would later criticize and ultimately reject.

At fourteen, Nietzsche earned a scholarship to Schulpforta, one of Germany's most prestigious boarding schools. The rigourous classical education he received there exposed him to ancient Greek and Roman texts, which would impact his philosophy.

However, his years at Schulpforta were socially isolating. Nietzsche was introverted and avoided the camaraderie of his peers, preferring solitary reflection. This early sense of estrangement shaped his intellectual independence and set the stage for his later critiques of conformity and 'herd mentality'.

Despite excelling academically, Nietzsche's formative years were characterized by a tension between the strict religiosity of his upbringing and his growing doubts about faith. His exposure to the works of Goethe, Schiller and the philosophers of antiquity sowed the seeds of his eventual rebellion against Christian dogma and his pursuit of intellectual freedom.

Nietzsche's intellectual journey continued at the Universities of Bonn and Leipzig, where he initially studied theology before shifting to philology, the study of language and texts. At Leipzig, Nietzsche encountered the pessimistic philosophy of Arthur Schopenhauer, whose ideas about the primacy of will and the futility of existence resonated with Nietzsche's emerging worldview. He also discovered the music of Richard Wagner, whose operas inspired Nietzsche with their blend of myth, emotion and cultural critique.

In 1869, at just twenty-four years old, Nietzsche was appointed professor of classical philology at the University of Basel in Switzerland, an achievement that highlighted his precocious talent. However, his academic career was short-lived. Nietzsche's dissatisfaction with the narrow confines of philology and his deteriorating health led him to resign in 1879. This decision freed him to focus entirely on his philosophical writings.

His ideas were often misunderstood during his lifetime, and he suffered a mental breakdown in his final years. His early works, such as *The Birth of Tragedy* (1872), reflected his fascination with Greek culture and its duality of Apollonian order and Dionysian chaos.

This theme of tension between opposing forces – reason and instinct, individual and collective – would permeate his later works, including *Beyond Good and Evil* and *Thus Spoke Zarathustra*. His contributions as an original thinker lay in his ability to critique traditional values while proposing bold, transformative ideas about human potential and creativity.

### Core Contribution to Political Philosophy

Nietzsche is best known for his analyses of traditional morality and religion. He believed that without religion, humanity lacked a clear sense of meaning and purpose and that individuals must create their own values to fill this void.

### The Effect of the Quote 'God is Dead'

Nietzsche's declaration that 'God is dead' is one of the most provocative and influential statements in modern philosophy. Introduced in *The Gay Science* and expanded in *Thus Spoke Zarathustra*, it encapsulates the cultural and moral crisis of his era. Nietzsche argued that the Enlightenment, with its stress on reason and science, had eroded faith in religious and metaphysical absolutes. Without God, humanity was left to confront a world devoid of inherent purpose.

This existential void, Nietzsche warned, could lead to nihilism – a state where life is perceived as meaningless. However, he also saw it as an opportunity for renewal. By rejecting inherited beliefs, individuals could create their own values and embrace life's uncertainties. Nietzsche's concept of the Übermensch represented this ideal of self-overcoming, challenging humanity to rise above mediocrity and invent new ways of living.

'Übermensch' ('Overman' or 'Superman') is a person who transcends conventional morality and embraces life-affirming values. The Übermensch represents radical self-overcoming, striving to become the fullest expression of human potential through the 'will to power', which he saw as the fundamental drive for growth, creativity and self-mastery.

The impact of this idea extended far beyond philosophy. Existentialist thinkers like Jean-Paul Sartre and Albert Camus drew on Nietzsche's insights to explore themes of freedom, responsibility and the absurd. In literature, Nietzsche influenced figures like James Joyce and Franz Kafka, while his critique of traditional morality continues to resonate in debates about ethics and individualism.

Nietzsche also evaluated the idea of objective truth. He argued that what we consider truth is often a social construct shaped by power dynamics. His work *On the Genealogy of Morals* explores the origins of moral values, contrasting 'master morality' (which values strength, creativity and nobility) with 'slave morality' (which values humility, meekness and obedience). Nietzsche saw the rise of Christianity and other moral systems as a form of slave morality that suppressed human vitality and creativity.

### Elisabeth Förster-Nietzsche and Her Influence

Elisabeth Förster-Nietzsche, Friedrich's younger sister, played a controversial role in shaping his posthumous reputation. Raised alongside Friedrich in their pious household, Elisabeth shared her brother's intellectual curiosity but diverged sharply in her ideological beliefs. While Friedrich rejected nationalism and anti-Semitism, Elisabeth embraced both with fervour.

In 1886, Elisabeth married Bernhard Förster, an anti-Semitic agitator, and joined him in founding an 'Aryan' colony in Paraguay. The colony failed disastrously, and Förster committed suicide, leaving Elisabeth disillusioned but unrepentant. After Nietzsche's mental collapse in 1889, Elisabeth returned to Germany and took control of his literary estate.

Elisabeth heavily edited and misrepresented Nietzsche's works, aligning them with her nationalist and anti-Semitic agenda. She compiled *The Will to Power*, a collection of Nietzsche's unpublished notes, into a pseudo-philosophical manifesto that he had never intended. Elisabeth also cultivated relationships with prominent Nazis, including Adolf Hitler, promoting Nietzsche as a philosophical precursor to their ideology.

However, Nietzsche's writings reveal his opposition to nationalism, anti-Semitism and authoritarianism. He criticized German chauvinism and described anti-Semites as 'buffoons'. Modern scholarship has exposed Elisabeth's distortions, restoring Nietzsche's reputation as a thinker who championed individuality and freedom.

### The Significance of *Thus Spoke Zarathustra*

*Thus Spoke Zarathustra* is Nietzsche's most celebrated work, blending philosophy, poetry and allegory in a narrative that follows Zarathustra, a fictional prophet. Written between 1883 and 1885, the book encapsulates Nietzsche's central themes:

**The Death of God:** Zarathustra proclaims the death of God, challenging humanity to face the implications of a world without divine purpose.

**The Übermensch:** It represents humanity's potential to transcend mediocrity, creating new values and embracing life with courage and creativity.

**Eternal Recurrence:** This thought experiment asks readers to imagine reliving their lives infinitely, emphasizing the importance of living authentically.

**The Three Metamorphoses:** Zarathustra describes the evolution of the human spirit through three stages: the camel (bearing burdens), the lion (rebelling against constraints) and the child (creating new values).

*Thus Spoke Zarathustra* has substantially impacted philosophy, literature and art. Martin Heidegger praised it as a transformative meditation on being while Richard Strauss's symphonic tone poem immortalized its themes in music. The book's aphoristic style and poetic depth continue to captivate readers, offering timeless insights into human existence.

### Nietzsche's Political Leanings and Misinterpretations

Nietzsche was an ardent critic of nationalism, anti-Semitism and mass movements, which he viewed as manifestations of herd mentality. His disdain for democracy and socialism stemmed from their tendency to suppress individual excellence in favour of mediocrity. Nietzsche championed the self-overcoming individual who could rise above societal constraints to create their own values.

However, Nietzsche's philosophy was misinterpreted and misappropriated by authoritarian regimes, particularly the Nazis. The concept of the Übermensch was distorted into a justification for Aryan supremacy, while his critique of Christian morality was twisted to support anti-Semitism. These distortions were largely the result of Elisabeth's editing and the selective reading of his works by Nazi ideologues.

Modern scholars point out that Nietzsche's philosophy celebrates individuality and creativity, opposing any form of collectivism or racial superiority.

## ANECDOTES

### 1. The Break with Wagner: From Devotion to Disillusionment

Friedrich Nietzsche initially idolized Richard Wagner, seeing him as a revolutionary force in art and philosophy. Wagner, in turn, saw Nietzsche as a brilliant disciple. Their friendship flourished, with Nietzsche frequently visiting Wagner's home and even dedicating *The Birth of Tragedy* (1872) to him.

However, Nietzsche grew disillusioned with Wagner's increasing nationalism, anti-Semitism and return to Christian themes in his later operas. By 1878, Nietzsche publicly broke with Wagner, criticizing him in *Human, All Too Human*. This rupture marked Nietzsche's shift away from Romanticism towards a more individualistic, iconoclastic philosophy.

### 2. The Solitary Wanderer: Writing in Isolation

After leaving academia, Nietzsche led a nomadic existence, moving between Switzerland, Italy and France in search of a climate that would ease his chronic illnesses. He lived in near-total isolation, writing feverishly and producing masterpieces such as *Thus Spoke Zarathustra*, *Beyond Good and Evil* and *The Genealogy of Morals*.

This self-imposed exile shaped his philosophy; his writings celebrated solitude, self-mastery and the rejection of societal norms. His suffering was not just physical but existential, fuelling his radical ideas about the will to power and the revaluation of values.

### 3. The Turin Epiphany: The Collapse of a Genius

In January 1889, Nietzsche suffered a mental breakdown in Turin, Italy. According to legend, he witnessed a horse being whipped in the street, ran to embrace it and collapsed in tears. This event is sometimes interpreted as a moment of deep existential anguish.

Shortly after, he began sending bizarre letters signed as 'Dionysus' and 'The Crucified'. His descent into madness ended his productive life. The Nietzschean themes of suffering, transcendence and the limits of human reason took on a tragic, personal dimension.

### 4. Nietzsche's Legacy Manipulated

After Nietzsche's death in 1900, his sister, Elisabeth Förster-Nietzsche, took control of his works. A devoted nationalist and anti-Semite, she selectively edited his writings, distorting his ideas to align with far-right ideology. She presented Nietzsche as a forerunner of German nationalism, paving the way for later misinterpretations by the Nazi regime.

In reality, Nietzsche despised nationalism, anti-Semitism and herd mentality. His legacy of radical individualism and critique of power was reshaped into something he likely would have abhorred. The irony of this posthumous betrayal reflects Nietzsche's warnings about the dangers of ideology and manipulation.

### Why His Ideas Matter Today

Friedrich Nietzsche's philosophy remains relevant in modern debates on individualism, morality and meaning in a secular world. His concepts of the Übermensch and 'will to power' have shaped existentialist thought, influencing figures like Jean-Paul Sartre and Albert Camus, who explored human freedom and self-creation in an indifferent universe.

His critique of traditional values laid the groundwork for modern cultural criticism, particularly in postmodern and deconstructionist thought. Thinkers like Michel Foucault drew on Nietzsche's ideas to challenge power structures and question the foundations of knowledge. His exploration of power, creativity and self-determination continues to influence contemporary discussions on identity, ethics and the role of the individual in society.

In an age of social media conformity, Nietzsche's critique of herd mentality feels more relevant than ever, while his emphasis on self-overcoming challenges passive approaches to personal growth. His philosophy offers a framework for those seeking meaning and authenticity in an uncertain world.

Despite the distortions of his ideas over time, Nietzsche's legacy endures as a philosopher of transformation, one who urges individuals to confront life's uncertainties with courage, creativity and a relentless pursuit of self-renewal.

## JOHN LOCKE: THE FATHER OF LIBERALISM

### Historical Context and Introduction

John Locke was born in England in 1632, during a time of political and religious turmoil, including the English Civil War and the Glorious Revolution.

The Civil War (1642–51) ended with the execution of Charles I (1649) and the rise of Oliver Cromwell's Puritan Commonwealth (1649–660), challenging entrenched notions of monarchy. The Restoration (1660), or the return of Charles II to the throne, marked the reassertion of monarchical power, but tensions regarding religious dissent and constitutional governance persisted. The Glorious Revolution (1688), or the overthrow of James II, a Catholic monarch, and ascension of William III and Mary II ushered in constitutional monarchy. This revolution solidified Locke's belief in limited government and provided the backdrop of his most influential works, including *Two Treatise of Government.*

Religious conflict between Protestants and Catholics dominated the century. Locke's Protestant upbringing and the persecution of dissenters under James II reinforced his commitment to religious toleration, which became a cornerstone of his philosophy.

Locke's lifetime coincided with the rise of empiricism and scientific inquiry, championed by thinkers like Francis Bacon (1561–1626) and Isaac Newton (1643–1727). This intellectual climate encouraged Locke to emphasize reason and observation, laying the foundation for his epistemology.

As a philosopher, his ideas shaped modern liberal thought, especially individual rights, government by consent and the separation of powers. His work laid the foundation for many democratic principles that influence politics today.

## Brief Biography

Locke's father, a lawyer and staunch Parliamentarian, supported Cromwell's cause during the English Civil War. His commitment to parliamentary sovereignty deeply influenced Locke's political philosophy, particularly his belief in accountable governance. Locke's family instilled in him a strong sense of moral responsibility, which became central to his works.

Locke excelled in classical studies, mastering Latin and Greek. Exposure to Stoic philosophy, particularly the works of Cicero, shaped his understanding of natural law and virtue. He studied medicine and philosophy at Oxford. Although he initially pursued a career in medicine, he was passionate about philosophy and political theory.

Locke was influenced and mentored by the likes of Robert Boyle, father of modern chemistry, Thomas Sydenham, a physician, and Anthony Ashley Cooper, 1st earl of Shaftesbury, with whom he gained first-hand experience in political governance and constitutional debates.

Locke's views on natural rights, that is, life, liberty and property, would later inspire Thomas Jefferson and the framers of the US Constitution. Locke spent much of his life in exile, during which time he continued to write and shape political theory.

## Core Contribution to Political Philosophy

John Locke's contributions reshaped epistemology, political philosophy, education and religious thought, earning him the title of the 'Father of Liberalism'.

### *An Essay Concerning Human Understanding* (1689)

In this seminal work, Locke rejected innate ideas, arguing that the mind at birth is a tabula rasa (blank slate) and that all knowledge arises from experience.

Locke divided knowledge into sensation (external experience) and reflection (internal processing), laying the foundation for modern psychology and epistemology. His critique of innate ideas challenged thinkers like René Descartes, emphasizing that knowledge must be tested and observed.

Locke's empiricism influenced Enlightenment thinkers, including David Hume and Immanuel Kant, shifting philosophy from speculation to the study of human experience. His theories underpin modern education systems, stressing experiential learning over rote memorization.

### *Two Treatises of Government* (1689)

Locke's political masterpiece, written during his exile in Holland, laid the groundwork for constitutional democracy and rejected the divine right of kings. Some of the key ideas he explored are:

1. Natural Rights: All individuals possess inherent rights to life, liberty and property.
2. Social Contract: Governments derive legitimacy from the consent of the governed and exist to protect natural rights.

3. Right to Revolution: Citizens have a moral duty to overthrow governments that violate their rights.

Locke's principles directly influenced Thomas Jefferson's Declaration of Independence during the American Revolution of 1776. During the French Revolution, his ideas inspired demands for liberty and equality. His emphasis on accountability and individual rights continues to influence constitutional democracies.

### *A Letter Concerning Toleration* (1689)

Locke advocated for religious pluralism, arguing that faith is a personal matter beyond the jurisdiction of the state.

He criticized forced conversions and state-imposed religion, arguing that genuine belief cannot be coerced. However, his toleration excluded atheists (deemed morally unreliable) and Catholics (seen as politically subversive).

His ideas influenced the First Amendment to the US Constitution and remain central to debates on pluralism and secularism. His principles echo in global discussions about freedom of conscience and religious equality.

### *Some Thoughts Concerning Education* (1693)

Locke emphasized character development, practical learning and critical thinking. His ideas shaped progressive educational practices, influencing figures like Maria Montessori and promoting holistic, child-centred learning.

He also supported the separation of powers, ensuring the legislative, executive and judicial branches remain independent to prevent anyone from becoming too powerful. His idea that citizens have the right to overthrow a government that fails to protect their rights became a key principle in modern democracies.

## ANECDOTES

### 1. The Shaftesbury Connection (1666–83)

Locke served as secretary and personal physician to Anthony Ashley Cooper, 1st Earl of Shaftesbury, a prominent Whig politician who opposed absolutism and advocated for constitutional monarchy. Locke assisted in drafting the Fundamental Constitutions of Carolina (1669), which promoted religious toleration and property rights.

Shaftesbury's influence exposed Locke to real-world political challenges, inspiring his later works, including *Two Treatises of Government*. His involvement with the Whig movement deepened his commitment to limiting royal power and protecting individual freedoms.

### 2. The Rye House Plot and Exile in Holland (1683–89)

In 1683, Locke fled England after being implicated in the 'Rye House Plot', a failed conspiracy to assassinate Charles II and James II. He spent six years in Holland, surrounded by intellectuals, religious dissenters and political exiles, including the philosopher Pierre Bayle.

During his exile, Locke wrote *Two Treatises of Government* and *A Letter Concerning Toleration*, heavily influenced by the Dutch tradition of religious tolerance and political liberty. This period cemented his belief in government by consent and the separation of church and state.

### 3. The Glorious Revolution and Locke's Return (1688)

After the Glorious Revolution overthrew James II, Locke returned to England in 1689, welcomed by the new regime of William III and Mary II. His political philosophy aligned with the revolution's ideals, advocating for constitutional monarchy and the protection of individual rights.

The revolution provided the real-world context for Locke's *Two Treatises*, which justified the right to overthrow tyrannical rulers. His ideas shaped the English Bill of Rights (1689) and later influenced democratic revolutions, including the American and French Revolutions.

### 4. Locke's Role in the Board of Trade (1696–1700)

In his later years, Locke served on the Board of Trade, advising the government on colonial policies, trade regulations and economic reforms. He applied his theories on property rights and governance to real-world policymaking, influencing trade laws and colonial administration.

Locke's work at the Board demonstrated the practical application of his political philosophy. His ideas on property, liberty and governance later shaped debates leading to the American Revolution and influenced the development of modern capitalism.

### Why His Ideas Matter Today

John Locke's stress on natural rights, the social contract and government by consent has profoundly shaped modern liberal democracies, particularly in Western Europe and the United States.

His ideas on 'individual liberty, the separation of powers, and the right to revolt against unjust governments' continue to inform contemporary discussions on human rights, democracy and governance. In *Two Treatises of Government*, Locke argued that all humans possess fundamental freedoms of life, liberty and property, which governments exist to protect. He introduced the idea of a social contract, where people form a government to safeguard their rights in exchange for some personal freedoms. This framework remains central to modern political theory, influencing how societies structure governance, define rights and ensure justice.

Locke's concept of 'natural rights' directly inspired the Universal Declaration of Human Rights (1948) and continues to shape discussions on privacy rights, data protection and freedom of speech, particularly in societies facing authoritarian restrictions. His principles of government by consent and accountability underpin modern democratic institutions, influencing electoral reforms, proportional representation and constitutional limits on executive power, such as US impeachment debates. His vision of religious toleration resonates in ongoing discussions about secularism, freedom of conscience and protections for religious minorities, particularly in response to anti-Muslim and anti-Semitic policies worldwide.

Locke's theory of 'property and labour' remains central to modern conversations on wealth distribution, land rights and taxation. Issues like Indigenous land claims and environmental conservation reflect his ideas about ownership and the ethical use of resources. His principles also inform contemporary economic debates about taxation and economic fairness. Additionally, his belief in 'experiential learning and critical thinking' has shaped modern progressive education systems, such as Montessori and Waldorf schools.

## DR B.R. AMBEDKAR: THE ARCHITECT OF MODERN INDIAN DEMOCRACY

### Historical Context and Introduction

Dr Bhimrao Ramji Ambedkar, born on 14 April 1891, in Mhow (present-day Madhya Pradesh), was a revolutionary thinker and leader who rose from the marginalized Dalit community to become a principal architect of modern India. Ambedkar's legacy lies in his unyielding fight against caste-based discrimination, his seminal role in drafting the Indian Constitution and his broader vision for a society based on liberty, equality and fraternity.

During his lifetime, British India was a society deeply fractured by caste, class and colonial exploitation. Ambedkar's life and work were shaped by the harsh realities of caste discrimination and social exclusion that he experienced as a member of the 'untouchable' Dalit community.

While nationalist leaders like Gandhi and Nehru focused on ending British rule, he devoted his life to challenging social hierarchies, advocating for the rights of marginalized groups and shaping the legal and political landscape of independent India. His advocacy for the rights of Dalits, women and marginalized communities established him as one of the foremost political philosophers and social reformers of his time.

### Brief Biography

Dr Ambedkar's early life was defined by the stark realities of caste discrimination. Born into the Mahar caste, considered untouchable, he faced ostracism from a young age. For example, he was forced to sit outside the classroom on the floor while his upper-caste peers sat inside, and he was denied access to drinking water unless someone from a higher caste poured it for him.

Despite these challenges, his father, Ramji Sakpal, instilled in him the value of education. Ramji, a subedar in the British army, ensured that his children were educated despite societal prejudices.

Young Ambedkar excelled in studies and went on to earn many degrees from prestigious international institutions that took him far beyond the oppressive confines of India's caste system. After completing his degree in economics and political science at Bombay University, he won a scholarship to study at Columbia University in 1913. At Columbia, Ambedkar earned his MA and later a PhD for his groundbreaking thesis *The Evolution of Provincial Finance in British India*. During his time there, he was profoundly influenced by John Dewey, whose ideas on democracy and education shaped Ambedkar's own philosophy of social reform.

From Columbia, Ambedkar went to London, where he pursued further studies at the London School of Economics (LSE) and trained as a barrister at Gray's Inn. His years in England not only expanded his intellectual horizons but also deepened his commitment to addressing caste-based oppression. His study of political economy and constitutional law at LSE equipped him with tools to analyse and propose solutions for India's systemic inequalities.

Returning to India in 1923, Ambedkar plunged into the sociopolitical struggles of Dalits. He began advocating for their rights, challenging the systemic exclusion they faced in public spaces, education and politics. One of his most notable early campaigns was the Mahad Satyagraha (1927), where he led a protest demanding Dalits' right to access water from a public tank in Mahad, Maharashtra. This event became a symbol of the larger fight for Dalit dignity and equality.

Ambedkar also began publishing journals like *Mooknayak* and *Bahishkrit Bharat*, which highlighted the plight of marginalized communities and called for systemic reform. His sharp intellect and unwavering determination quickly made him a prominent voice for social justice.

He was instrumental in the abolition of untouchability and the establishment of policies that would provide equal opportunities for all citizens. He is remembered for his conversion to Buddhism in 1956 as an act of protest against the caste system and as a call for social and spiritual liberation.

Dr Ambedkar is most famous for his role in drafting the Constitution of India as the chairman of the Constitution Drafting Committee.

### Core Contribution to Political Philosophy

Dr Ambedkar's main contribution to political philosophy was his fight for social justice, equality and the protection of human rights. His work aimed to dismantle the caste system, which he saw as a major source of oppression and inequality in Indian society. Ambedkar argued for the recognition of human dignity and the need for constitutional safeguards to protect the rights of marginalized groups.

Ambedkar's criticism of the caste system was most powerfully articulated in his book *Annihilation of Caste* (1936). This fiery manifesto called for the complete dismantling of caste, which he saw as the greatest obstacle to India's progress. He argued that caste was not just a social evil but a deeply ingrained religious practice sanctioned by texts like the

*Manusmriti*. Ambedkar's public burning of the *Manusmriti* in 1927 symbolized his rejection of Hindu orthodoxy.

His analysis went beyond critique; Ambedkar proposed practical measures for reform, including education, inter-caste marriages and economic empowerment. His vision was not limited to Dalits; he sought a society where liberty, equality and fraternity were universal values.

**Creation of the Indian Constitution**

As the chief architect of the Indian Constitution, Dr Ambedkar created a legal framework that guaranteed equality, justice and the protection of rights for all citizens, irrespective of their caste, religion or gender.

He also introduced affirmative action policies, such as reservations for Dalits in education and government services, to address historical wrongs. Ambedkar lay emphasis on education, social reform and political participation as essential to achieving social justice.

His key contributions to the Constitution of India include the abolition of untouchability as stated in Article 17, a guarantee of equality before the law and protection from discrimination as a Fundamental Right of all citizens and the introduction of affirmative action policies like reservations in education, employment and legislatures for Scheduled Castes and Tribes. He was also instrumental in including the promotion of social welfare and economic justice as a Directive Principle of State Policy.

Ambedkar's work ensured that India's Constitution was not just a legal document but a blueprint for a just society.

### Advocacy for Women and Marginalized Communities

Ambedkar was a pioneer in advocating for women's rights. His work on the Hindu Code Bill sought to grant women equal rights in property, divorce and inheritance. Though the bill faced stiff opposition and was not passed during his lifetime, it laid the foundation for later reforms.

Ambedkar's broader vision for social justice included labour protections, access to education and improved living conditions for marginalized communities. His legislative efforts reflected his belief that true democracy required both political and social equality.

### Conversion to Buddhism: A Political Act

In 1956, Ambedkar and over 5,00,000 followers embraced Buddhism in a historic mass conversion. This act was a rejection of the caste hierarchy embedded in Hinduism and an affirmation of Buddhism's egalitarian values. Ambedkar's choice of Buddhism was deeply symbolic as it aligned with his principles of liberty, equality and fraternity. This movement continues to inspire Dalit communities in their fight for dignity and rights.

### Ambedkar in Popular Culture

Ambedkar's legacy endures in Indian culture and beyond. Films like *Dr Babasaheb Ambedkar* and numerous books have kept his memory alive. Statues of Ambedkar, often with a raised finger pointing to the Constitution, are ubiquitous across India, signifying his vision for justice.

### Global Influence and Legacy

Ambedkar's ideas resonate globally. His stress on human rights parallels the struggles of marginalized groups worldwide. Leaders like Martin Luther King Jr. drew inspiration from Ambedkar's approach to systemic reform, particularly his focus on legal and social equality.

## ANECDOTES

### 1. The Water Tank Protest (Mahad Satyagraha, 1927)

Ambedkar led thousands of Dalits to drink water from a public tank in Mahad, Maharashtra, challenging caste-based restrictions on access to common resources. What seemed like a simple act of drinking water became a powerful assertion of equality.

This protest was a turning point in the fight against untouchability. Ambedkar famously declared, 'We are not going to the tank to merely drink water. We are going to assert that we, too, are human beings.' The event demonstrated his ability to transform everyday injustices into political movements.

### 2. Burning of the *Manusmriti* (1927)

At the same Mahad gathering, Ambedkar publicly burned the *Manusmriti*, an ancient Hindu text that sanctioned caste discrimination. This act of defiance sent shockwaves across Indian society, directly challenging the religious basis of social hierarchy.

For Ambedkar, rejecting the *Manusmriti* was essential to dismantling the ideological foundation of untouchability. His bold stance reinforced his belief that social reform required both legal and cultural transformation.

### 3. Clash with Gandhi on Separate Electorates (1932)

Ambedkar advocated for separate electorates for Dalits to ensure their political representation, a stance that led to a direct confrontation with Mahatma Gandhi, who opposed the idea, fearing it would divide Hindu society.

The dispute culminated in the Poona Pact, where Ambedkar reluctantly agreed to reserved seats within the Hindu electorate instead of separate electorates. Though a compromise, Ambedkar remained sceptical about whether Dalits could achieve true political power under this system.

### 4. The Baroda Palace Incident (1917)

After completing his education, Ambedkar returned to India to serve as a finance officer in Baroda. Despite his qualifications, he faced discrimination from his colleagues, who refused to share office space or serve him water.

Unable to find housing due to his caste, Ambedkar had to leave Baroda. This humiliating experience reinforced his resolve to fight against untouchability, proving that education alone could not erase caste prejudice – it required systemic change.

### 5. Resignation Over the Hindu Code Bill (1951)

As India's first law minister, Ambedkar drafted the Hindu Code Bill, a progressive legal reform aimed at ensuring equal rights for women in marriage, inheritance and divorce. However, opposition from conservative lawmakers stalled its passage.

Frustrated by the lack of commitment to social reform, Ambedkar resigned from his ministerial post in 1951. His resignation speech was a scathing critique of the Indian government's unwillingness to challenge entrenched social inequalities.

**Why His Ideas Matter Today**

Dr B.R. Ambedkar's vision for social justice, human rights and equality remains extremely relevant in contemporary India and beyond. His fight against caste discrimination and his advocacy for a democratic society, where every individual, regardless of background, can live with dignity and freedom, continue to shape India's legal and political landscape. His role in drafting the Indian Constitution laid the foundation for a more inclusive society, and his call for social reform still echoes in movements demanding justice and equity.

His push for affirmative action transformed opportunities for marginalized communities, ensuring access to education, employment and political representation. While these policies have uplifted many, ongoing debates about their scope and effectiveness highlight the challenges in balancing historical redress with contemporary aspirations. Ambedkar's emphasis on education as a tool for empowerment remains crucial, with scholarships and government initiatives reflecting his belief in knowledge as the key to liberation.

Beyond India, Ambedkar's fight against systemic inequality aligns with global human rights movements, such as Black Lives Matter and Dalit Lives Matter, which challenge entrenched discrimination and advocate for dignity and justice. His critique of social hierarchies and his vision of liberty, equality and fraternity continue to inspire activists, policymakers and scholars worldwide.

While progress has been made, the persistence of caste-based violence and social inequality underscores the unfinished nature of Ambedkar's mission. His dream was not merely to reform laws but to transform society itself. His enduring relevance serves as a reminder that the fight for justice is ongoing – and that true social change requires continued commitment from all who seek a more just and equitable world.

## HANNAH ARENDT: THE THINKER OF TOTALITARIANISM, POWER AND FREEDOM

### Historical Context and Introduction

Hannah Arendt, born on 14 October 1906 in Linden, Germany, grew up in a world teetering on the brink of upheaval. Her formative years coincided with the collapse of empires after World War I, the Great Depression and the rise of ideologies like Nazism and communism that promised order in a fragmented world. These seismic shifts were not just background events; they directly shaped Arendt's intellectual pursuits and personal life.

As a Jewish child in Kaiser Wilhelm's Germany, Arendt experienced the subtle yet pervasive anti-Semitism of the time. However, it was during the 1930s, as the Nazi Party gained power, that this prejudice became a defining force in her life. The Nuremberg Laws systematically stripped Jews of citizenship and dignity, targeting intellectuals like Arendt. In 1933, she was arrested for collecting anti-Semitic propaganda for a Zionist group. Although she was released, this harrowing experience marked the beginning of her exile.

Fleeing first to France and later to the United States, Arendt's encounters with statelessness deeply influenced her thought. She once described the condition of being stateless as a loss of 'the right to have rights', a theme she later developed in *The Origins of Totalitarianism*. These personal struggles transformed her from a philosopher concerned with abstract questions into a political thinker dedicated to studying the forces that dehumanize individuals and societies.

Arendt explored the nature of totalitarianism, power and freedom, focusing on political responsibility and the importance of public engagement. Her works have had a lasting impact on political philosophy, especially in understanding the nature of modern politics, authority and the human condition in times of crisis.

## Brief Biography

Hannah Arendt's upbringing in a liberal Jewish household fostered her intellectual independence. After her father's death, her mother, Martha Cohn Arendt, took on the role of shaping her daughter's worldview. Martha, a fierce advocate for education and resilience, encouraged Hannah to read widely and think critically. This early environment of inquiry and defiance laid the groundwork for her later philosophical rigour.

Arendt studied philosophy in Germany, at the University of Marburg first and later at the University of Heidelberg. In the US, after fleeing the Nazis in 1941, she became a leading intellectual, contributing extensively to political theory, political philosophy and the analysis of totalitarianism.

Arendt excelled academically, immersing herself in literature and philosophy during her teenage years. Works by Kant, Goethe and Kierkegaard deeply impacted her, particularly their stress on autonomy, ethics and the human condition. Her early intellectual development, however, was not isolated from her experiences as a Jew in a predominantly Christian society. Arendt often reflected on how subtle social exclusions foreshadowed larger systems of dehumanization, an insight that would shape her later critique of totalitarianism.

Throughout her career, Arendt remained a fierce advocate for democracy and political engagement while simultaneously warning against the dangers of totalitarianism, bureaucracy and unchecked power. She was critical of both communism and fascism, believing that totalitarian ideologies stifled individual freedoms and autonomy. Arendt's intellectual legacy is shaped by her insistence on the importance of public action, the responsibility of citizens in political life and the need to preserve political plurality in democratic societies.

Her notable works include *The Origins of Totalitarianism*, *The Human Condition*, *The Banality of Evil* and *The Life of the Mind.*

## Core Contribution to Political Philosophy

Hannah Arendt was one of the most influential political thinkers of the twentieth century, known for her analysis of totalitarianism, power, authority and freedom. Her work reshaped political philosophy by emphasizing action, human plurality and the nature of the public sphere.

### *The Origins of Totalitarianism*

Arendt's landmark work, *The Origins of Totalitarianism*, examined how regimes like Nazi Germany and Stalinist

Russia emerged from the breakdown of traditional political structures and the alienation of individuals from public life. She argued that totalitarian regimes do not rely solely on terror but also on ideology, enforcing a single, all-encompassing worldview that erases independent thought. Her concept of the 'banality of evil', introduced in *Eichmann in Jerusalem*, further demonstrated how ordinary individuals can become complicit in extraordinary atrocities through blind obedience and moral abdication.

### *The Human Condition*

In *The Human Condition*, Arendt explored the nature of human activity and introduced the concept of 'vita activa', which she divided into three categories:

- Labour: The repetitive biological tasks necessary for survival.
- Work: The creation of durable objects that shape the world.
- Action: The highest form of human engagement, where individuals participate in the public sphere, shaping collective life through speech and decision-making.

For Arendt, true politics was about action and human interaction, rather than governance or statecraft. She believed that freedom emerged not from individual autonomy alone but from participation in public life and recognition by others.

### Intellectual Influences and Academic Journey

Arendt's philosophical journey began at the University of Marburg, where she studied under Martin Heidegger.

Heidegger introduced her to existentialism and the idea of being-in-the-world, which emphasized individual experience and authenticity. However, their romantic and philosophical relationship became severely strained due to his support for the Nazi Party. While she never publicly denounced his influence, she distanced herself from his ideology and later described his philosophy as 'contaminated' by political choices.

She later studied under Karl Jaspers at the University of Heidelberg, where she wrote her dissertation on Saint Augustine's concept of love. Though theological in nature, this early work hinted at her enduring interest in the relationship between individuality and community.

The rise of Nazism had a significant impact on Arendt's intellectual trajectory. Forced to flee Germany, she turned her focus from traditional metaphysical concerns to the urgent political crises of her time. Her experiences as a refugee and exile influenced her commitment to exploring power structures and statelessness. This experience also reinforced a crucial lesson: Philosophy divorced from ethical responsibility risks complicity in oppression. Her teaching approach encouraged students to critically engage with history and challenge dominant ideologies, a perspective shaped by her confrontation with Heidegger's moral failings.

### Challenging Traditional Political Thought

Arendt rejected conventional political theories that equated politics with governance or state power. Instead, she argued that politics is fundamentally about human interaction, speech and plurality – the space where individuals come together to debate and act.

Her criticism of both liberalism and Marxism was striking. Liberalism, she argued, overly stressed individual rights while neglecting collective political action. Marxism, with its focus on class struggle, ignored the importance of human plurality and the dynamics of real political engagement.

By redefining power as something that emerges from cooperation rather than domination, Arendt provided a radical and enduring vision of political life.

## A Woman in Political Philosophy

Arendt's success was extraordinary in a field dominated by men. Despite barriers in academia, she established herself as a formidable thinker through intellectual rigour and resilience. While she distanced herself from feminist movements of her time, her work addressed universal concerns of power, exclusion and political participation.

Her own experiences of being a Jewish refugee and a woman in exile informed her perspective on statelessness and human rights. She emphasized that politics must be rooted in the realities of human plurality, not abstract ideals of equality that ignore individual differences.

Arendt's insights continue to resonate today. Her concept of totalitarianism remains essential to understanding oppressive regimes, and her belief in the importance of public participation in politics serves as a crucial reminder of the responsibilities of citizenship. Her life and work exemplify the power of critical thought in confronting political crises, making her one of the most significant voices in modern political philosophy.

## ANECDOTES

### 1. The Eichmann Trial and the Banality of Evil

Arendt's coverage of Adolf Eichmann's trial in *Eichmann in Jerusalem* remains one of her most controversial works. She portrayed Eichmann not as a monstrous villain but as an unthinking bureaucrat and a man who committed atrocities not out of deep ideological hatred but out of blind obedience and thoughtlessness.

This concept of the banality of evil challenged conventional understandings of morality and responsibility, provoking a fierce backlash, especially from Holocaust survivors. Yet, for Arendt, the trial underscored a fundamental danger: the ease with which ordinary people could become complicit in horrific crimes.

### 2. Escape from Nazi Occupation

Arendt was arrested in France for her anti-Nazi activities and interned in the Gurs camp. Managing a daring escape, she crossed the Pyrenees on foot and navigated the perils of wartime Europe, eventually securing passage to the United States.

This experience shaped her understanding of statelessness and the vulnerability of refugees. She later wrote extensively about the fragility of human rights when people have no nation to claim them.

### 3. Confrontation with Heidegger

Arendt had a complex relationship with her former mentor and lover, Martin Heidegger, who became entangled with the Nazi Party. Despite his intellectual influence on her, she refused to excuse his moral and political failings.

Decades after the war, she met with Heidegger again, leading to an uneasy reconciliation. However, she remained deeply critical of intellectuals who detached themselves from political responsibility – a theme that permeated much of her work on totalitarianism and moral accountability.

### 4. The Hannah Arendt Affair at the New School

As a professor at the New School in New York, Arendt was known for her sharp intellect and rigourous debates. However, her views on race and civil rights were controversial, particularly when she questioned forced integration in US schools, arguing that social change should not come through state coercion.

This stance alienated some of her progressive allies, leading to fierce academic debates. Arendt's willingness to challenge even dominant liberal narratives exemplified her intellectual independence. She never aligned herself fully with any political ideology, valuing critical thought above all.

## Why Her Ideas Matter Today

Hannah Arendt's philosophy remains very relevant in contemporary discussions on authoritarianism, individual responsibility in political life and the preservation of democratic freedoms. Her warnings about totalitarianism resonate strongly in an era of political extremism, populism and rising illiberal regimes. In an age of polarization, her advocacy for dialogue, cooperation and political pluralism offers a crucial framework for sustaining democracy.

Her concept of the banality of evil serves as a powerful reminder of the dangers of complacency and the necessity of vigilance in the face of injustice. As digital surveillance expands and democratic institutions face increasing threats, Arendt's insights into power, authoritarianism and human rights carry renewed urgency. She championed the public sphere as a space for collective action, countering the isolating effects of modern technology and political divisions.

Arendt's legacy as a political philosopher is defined by her fearless examination of power, human rights and the conditions for a thriving public life. Shaped by her experiences as a Jewish exile and a woman in a male-dominated field, her work remains unparalleled in its depth and relevance. Her stress on action, plurality and critical thinking continues to inspire, urging us to confront the complexities of political life with courage and integrity.

More than just evaluating history's darkest chapters, she envisioned a politics rooted in human dignity and collective responsibility, an enduring call to engage with the world thoughtfully and decisively.

## EMMA GOLDMAN: THE VOICE OF ANARCHISM AND REVOLUTIONARY THOUGHT

### Historical Context and Introduction

Emma Goldman was born on 27 June 1869 in Kovno, Lithuania, then part of the Russian Empire under Tsar Alexander II. Her early life was shaped by the intersection of multiple oppressive systems: the autocratic rule of the tsar, the pervasive anti-Semitism that marginalized Jewish communities and rigid gender roles that limited women's opportunities.

Lithuania, in the nineteenth century, was under Russian imperial rule, a period marked by political repression, forced Russification and the denial of national and cultural rights. Goldman's family lived in the Pale of Settlement, a territory designated for Jews by the Russian Empire.

Jews were barred from living in major cities, owning land or participating in many professions. Institutionalized discrimination, including pogroms (violent anti-Jewish riots), frequently terrorized Jewish communities. In nearby regions, pogroms in Odessa (1871) and Kishinev (1903) left devastating psychological scars on Jews throughout the empire.

Despite systemic discrimination, Jewish communities resisted by fostering strong networks of education and mutual aid, often rooted in religious traditions.

As a young woman, she moved to the United States and became one of the most prominent anarchists and political activists of her time. She was influenced by the tumultuous events of the late nineteenth and early twentieth centuries, such as labour strikes, the women's suffrage movement and the rise of industrial capitalism. Her work challenged the very foundation of traditional authority, whether political, social or economic, and advocated for a world built on voluntary cooperation and individual freedom.

As a speaker, writer and activist, Goldman strongly opposed both capitalism and state authority. She called for radical change through direct action and saw anarchism as the means to create a society based on equality, freedom and solidarity. Although controversial in her time, Goldman's ideas shaped modern political activism. Her critiques of state power, gender inequality and capitalism continue to influence social movements to this day.

**Brief Biography**

Goldman's family, like many Jewish families, was subjected to institutional and social anti-Semitism. They lived in constant fear of violence and dispossession. Jews were prohibited from attending universities or working in certain trades, forcing families like Goldman's to rely on precarious livelihoods. Goldman's father, a traditional and authoritarian man, struggled to provide for the family, often blaming their difficulties on external discrimination. This precarious existence fostered Goldman's deep-seated awareness of systemic oppression.

Goldman's early life was further constrained by traditional gender expectations within both Lithuanian and Jewish societies. Her father believed a woman's role was confined to the domestic sphere. He reportedly said, 'All a girl needs to know is how to make gefilte fish,' dismissing Goldman's desire for education.

Goldman's frustration with these limitations sparked her defiance against patriarchal norms. She refused to accept the life of subservience her father envisioned, planting the seeds of her feminist consciousness.

The economic hardships faced by Goldman's family were a result of both systemic discrimination and the collapse of local industries. The Industrial Revolution bypassed rural Lithuania, leaving many Jewish families impoverished and dependent on small-scale trades.

The promise of economic stability and freedom in the United States attracted Jewish families, including Goldman's, who sought to escape persecution and build better lives.

In 1885, at the age of sixteen, Goldman emigrated with her sister to join family members in Rochester, New York. The journey itself was arduous, reflecting the desperation and determination of immigrants seeking refuge from oppression.

Arriving in America, Goldman encountered the stark reality of industrial exploitation in the land of supposed freedom. She initially worked in factories before becoming deeply involved in political activism.

A fierce advocate for anarchism, labour rights, women's liberation and free speech, she was instrumental in the development of radical leftist thought during the early twentieth century.

Known for her eloquent speeches and sharp critiques of social structures, Goldman was a leader in the anarchist movement. However, her views on violence, revolution and state power sometimes caused friction with other activists.

Goldman travelled extensively and often faced persecution for her views. She was arrested multiple times for her speeches, writings and involvement in political actions, including her support for the Haymarket Affair and the campaign for free speech. In 1919, Goldman was deported from the United States due to her activism and lived the remainder of her life in various countries, including Canada, Russia and France, before passing away in 1940.

## Core Contribution to Political Philosophy

Emma Goldman's intellectual journey is as remarkable as her activism. Growing up in a society that denied women formal education and opportunities, she became a self-taught thinker through relentless determination and an insatiable thirst for knowledge. Her transformation from an uneducated factory worker to one of the most influential anarchist philosophers of her time is a testament to her resilience and passion for justice.

### Intellectual Growth and Education

Goldman's education was both self-driven and action-oriented. Despite long working hours, she borrowed books, frequented libraries and immersed herself in radical bookstores in New York's Lower East Side. Influenced by thinkers like Friedrich Nietzsche, John Stuart Mill and Henry David Thoreau, her intellectual rebellion paralleled her defiance of gendered expectations.

However, Goldman's learning extended beyond books. Organizing strikes, delivering speeches and engaging in debates sharpened her understanding of political and social structures. Her experiences interacting with workers and intellectuals refined her rhetorical skills and deepened her grasp of anarchist philosophy.

### Advocacy for Anarchism

Goldman's primary contribution to political philosophy was her advocacy for anarchism, which she saw as more than just opposition to government. She believed true freedom required dismantling oppressive social structures, including patriarchy, capitalism and organized religion.

Her vision of anarchism emphasized:

- Personal autonomy and voluntary cooperation: Promoting self-governance over state control.

- Mutual aid: Advocating for community-driven solutions instead of hierarchical systems.
- Direct action: Encouraging protests, strikes and civil disobedience as necessary tools for social change.

Unlike many political thinkers of her time, Goldman also championed personal freedoms, particularly for women. She underlined their right to make choices about their bodies, relationships and societal roles – ideas that later influenced feminist movements.

**Challenging Traditional Beliefs**

Goldman defied the norms of her time with radical critiques of capitalism, marriage and state authority.

1. Capitalism and Economic Exploitation: Goldman exposed the systemic inequalities of industrial capitalism, calling it a system built on the exploitation of the working class. She highlighted the plight of sweatshop workers and child labourers, delivering speeches in industrial hubs like New York and Chicago. Her critiques laid the groundwork for modern labour movements and economic justice debates.
2. Marriage as Bondage: In her essay 'Marriage and Love', Goldman argued that marriage commodified women, reducing them to economic dependents. Her criticism influenced later feminists like Betty Friedan and Adrienne Rich, who further deconstructed traditional gender roles.
3. Birth Control and Women's Autonomy: Goldman's 1916 arrest for distributing birth control literature

spotlighted the need for reproductive rights. Her advocacy inspired figures like Margaret Sanger and laid the foundation for the modern reproductive justice movement.

### Disillusionment with Marxism

Goldman's time in Soviet Russia (1920–21) exposed her to the authoritarianism of Marxist rule. Witnessing the brutal suppression of the Kronstadt Rebellion (1921), where sailors demanded free speech and economic reform, solidified her critique of state socialism.

Her meeting with Lenin further reinforced her belief that true liberation could not be achieved through centralized power. This prescient analysis foreshadowed later disillusionment with totalitarian regimes across the twentieth century.

### Contribution to Feminist Political Philosophy

Goldman's feminist philosophy was revolutionary, merging personal autonomy with political resistance long before it became a core tenet of feminist thought.

1. Marriage and Gender Roles: She deconstructed marriage as an institution of economic and emotional dependency, prefiguring second-wave feminism's critique of domestic oppression.
2. Sexual Freedom and Birth Control: Goldman linked sexual autonomy to broader social liberation, highlighting women's right to control their own bodies. These ideas influenced the sexual revolution and modern reproductive justice movements.

3. Intersectionality: Goldman recognized oppression as multifaceted, connecting gender inequality with class exploitation and state repression. Her holistic approach anticipated the principles of contemporary intersectional feminism.

## ANECDOTES

### 1. Free Speech Advocacy

In 1908, Emma Goldman embarked on a cross-country speaking tour to defend free speech, facing intense police censorship. In cities like Chicago and San Francisco, authorities shut down her meetings, arrested her supporters and tried to silence her by force.

Goldman's persistence drew national attention to the principle of free expression. Her advocacy laid the groundwork for future legal battles over free speech and influenced the formation of the American Civil Liberties Union (ACLU), which later championed First Amendment rights.

### 2. Arrest for Birth Control Advocacy

In 1916, she was arrested in New York for distributing information on contraception, which was illegal under the Comstock Laws. Despite public outcry, she was sentenced to prison, becoming one of the first high-profile activists to face legal consequences for promoting reproductive rights.

Her arrest brought national attention to the birth control movement, paving the way for figures like Margaret Sanger and the eventual legalization of contraceptive access.

Goldman's fight for reproductive autonomy remains a cornerstone of feminist activism.

### 3. Deportation from the United States in 1919

During the First Red Scare, Goldman and fellow anarchist Alexander Berkman were deported under the Anarchist Exclusion Act. Branded a dangerous radical, she was forcibly sent to Soviet Russia, marking the US government's aggressive crackdown on anarchist movements.

Despite losing her platform in the United States, Goldman continued her activism abroad, becoming a global advocate for anarchism and human rights. Her deportation underscored the government's fear of radical ideas and remains a pivotal moment in US history.

### 4. Meeting Lenin and the Kronstadt Rebellion

Initially supportive of the Bolshevik Revolution, Goldman moved to Soviet Russia in 1920, believing it aligned with her radical ideals. However, a meeting with Vladimir Lenin revealed deep ideological divides – when she questioned the suppression of dissent, Lenin dismissed free speech as a 'bourgeois luxury'.

The 1921 Kronstadt Rebellion, led by sailors demanding political freedoms, became a turning point. The Bolsheviks brutally crushed the uprising, killing thousands. Disillusioned, Goldman concluded that centralized, authoritarian systems, even socialist ones, were inherently oppressive, a criticism that continues to resonate.

### 5. Spanish Civil War Advocacy (1936–39)

During the Spanish Civil War, Goldman actively supported anarchist forces fighting against Francisco Franco's fascist regime. She organized international aid, delivered passionate speeches and wrote extensively about the struggle, rallying global support for the anarchist cause.

Goldman's work highlighted her unwavering commitment to combating authoritarianism in all its forms. Her efforts inspired later anti-fascist movements and reinforced the importance of international solidarity in the fight against oppression.

## JOHN RAWLS: THE ARCHITECT OF MODERN POLITICAL JUSTICE

### Historical Context and Introduction

John Rawls was born on 21 February 1921 in Baltimore, Maryland, into an affluent family with a strong commitment to education and civic responsibility. The interwar period during which Rawls grew up was marked by significant economic and political upheavals, including the Great Depression (1929–39) and rising tensions leading to World War II (1939–45).

The Great Depression exposed severe economic disparities and social inequalities across the United States. Although Rawls' family was shielded from financial hardship, these disparities likely shaped his sensitivity to issues of justice and fairness. Growing up in Maryland, a border state with deep racial segregation, he witnessed the entrenched systemic inequalities of pre-Civil Rights America.

These turbulent times highlighted the need for fair and just political structures that could ensure peace and equality in societies. Rawls aimed to balance individual freedoms with social justice, especially in addressing inequality.

His seminal work, *A Theory of Justice*, redefined how we think about justice in a modern liberal democracy. Rawls' ideas responded to key political and moral issues of his time, such as civil rights, economic inequality and the tension between personal liberty and government control. He sought to establish a fair framework to distribute resources and opportunities in society, guiding policies towards greater justice.

### Brief Biography

Rawls' youth coincided with the rise of totalitarian regimes and the increasing polarization between democracy, fascism and communism. These competing ideologies not only shaped global politics but also laid the groundwork for his focus on justice as a unifying framework for democratic societies.

His upbringing was marked by personal loss. Two of his younger brothers died from illnesses they contracted from him, which left a deep emotional impact. These experiences heightened his sensitivity to the arbitrary nature of suffering and shaped his focus on impartiality in the design of social systems.

Rawls' formative years of learning and education were marked by intellectual curiosity and academic rigour. After graduating from the Kent School in Connecticut, he enrolled at Princeton University in 1939, where he pursued a degree in philosophy. His time at Princeton was pivotal in shaping his philosophical outlook as he encountered the ideas of Immanuel Kant (1724–1804) and Henry Sidgwick (1838–1900), both of whom deeply influenced his later work on justice and fairness.

Rawls entered Princeton during an era of significant philosophical evolution. The analytical tradition in philosophy was gaining prominence, emphasizing clarity, logic and ethical inquiry. He excelled in his studies and was known for his ability to dissect complex ideas.

Princeton exposed him to a range of thinkers and debates on moral and political philosophy. It was during the same time that global conflict was intensifying, which led to the outbreak of World War II (1939), influencing much of the academic discourse, with debates focusing on justice, governance and human rights.

Rawls later became a professor at Harvard University, where he gained influence as a thinker and teacher. His early experiences during the Great Depression and World War II led him to ask fundamental questions about justice and fairness.

Rawls built a systematic approach to political theory, concentrating on justice as fairness. Besides *A Theory of Justice*, he wrote *Political Liberalism* and *The Law of Peoples*, expanding on justice and international relations.

### Core Contribution to Political Philosophy

John Rawls' most significant contribution to political philosophy was his theory of 'justice as fairness'. He argued that justice should be understood in terms of fairness and developed a framework for achieving the fair distribution of goods and opportunities in society. Central to his theory was the 'original position', a hypothetical scenario in which individuals choose principles of justice behind a 'veil of ignorance', ensuring impartiality by making decisions without knowledge of their own social status, wealth or abilities.

Rawls proposed two key principles of justice:

1. The Equal Liberty Principle: Everyone should have the same basic freedoms, provided they do not restrict others' freedoms.
2. The Difference Principle: Social and economic inequalities should benefit the least advantaged members of society.

This structured approach to fairness and equality distinguished Rawls from earlier liberal thinkers, who often overlooked society's most vulnerable.

**Influences on Rawls' Thought**

**Immanuel Kant (1724–1804):** Kant's moral philosophy was a cornerstone of Rawls' intellectual foundation. Kant's deontological ethics, particularly the concept of the categorical imperative, resonated with Rawls' pursuit of universal principles for justice. Kant's emphasis on autonomy and mortal agency directly influenced Rawls' idea of the veil of ignorance, where individuals design societal principles free from self-interest.

**Henry Sidgwick (1838–1900):** Sidgwick's utilitarian ethics also played a critical role in Rawls' intellectual development. In *The Methods of Ethics* (1874), Sidgwick sought to reconcile utilitarianism with common-sense morality, highlighting impartiality and moral equality. Although Rawls ultimately rejected utilitarianism, he appreciated Sidgwick's analytical rigour and focus on impartiality. Unlike Sidgwick, Rawls argued that utilitarianism's emphasis on aggregate happiness often overlooked individual rights, which led him to develop justice as fairness.

## Early Ethical Inquiry and War Experience

Rawls' senior thesis at Princeton reflected his early interest in ethical theory. His academic mentors encouraged him to explore questions of morality, autonomy and justice, setting the stage for his later work.

In 1943, Rawls enlisted in the US Army and served in the Pacific Theater, participating in the Battle of Leyte (1944). This experience of combat and the accompanying moral failures of war had a deep impact on his philosophical outlook.

While Rawls primarily served in the Pacific, he was intensely aware of the Nazi regime's policies, including its genocidal campaign against Jews, Romani people and other marginalized groups in Europe. Although no direct writings from this period survive, it is evident from his later work that Rawls was extremely disturbed by the implications of Hitler's policies and the Holocaust.

The Holocaust (1941–45), which resulted in the systematic extermination of approximately six million Jews, revealed to Rawls the dangers of unchecked power and ideological extremism. He saw it as the ultimate failure of a society to uphold the dignity and rights of individuals. The horrors of the Holocaust reinforced his belief that justice must prioritize the protection of individual rights over collective interests. His rejection of utilitarianism, because it could theoretically justify atrocities in the name of the 'greater good', is deeply tied to these observations.

Although Rawls rarely discussed the Holocaust explicitly in his later works, its influence is implicit in his emphasis on universal principles of justice and his critiques of moral relativism. The Holocaust served as a stark reminder that societies must be structured to prevent atrocities by ensuring that no group is dehumanized or excluded from the moral community.

During his service, Rawls also wrestled with questions about theodicy – the justification of divine justice in the face of evil. Witnessing the brutalities of war and the genocide in Europe led him to reject religious explanations for suffering. This rejection of theodicy influenced his decision to develop a secular moral framework for justice, one grounded in reason and human dignity, rather than divine authority.

Rawls' war experiences instilled in him a lifelong commitment to fairness and the protection of human rights. His exposure to systemic injustice during the war helped shape the foundation of his later works, particularly *The Veil of Ignorance* and *Justice as Fairness.*

### Rawls' Global Justice and Focus on National Systems

John Rawls' work primarily centred on domestic systems of justice, reflecting his focus on the structures and institutions of individual nations. In his seminal work, *A Theory of Justice* (1971), Rawls explicitly framed his principles of justice as fairness within the boundaries of a single democratic society. His choice to focus on national systems rather than global ones has sparked both admiration and criticism within the field of political philosophy.

Rawls believed that principles of justice were best applied to the basic structure of society, which he defined as the overarching institutions – legal, economic and political – that shape individuals' opportunities and interactions.

His reasoning for this focus included cohesive political communities, where shared political institutions, laws and norms provide the foundation for individuals to agree on principles of justice. And pluralism and the limits of global consensus, thereby acknowledging the challenges of applying universal principles of justice in a world divided by diverse cultures, religions and political ideologies. He believed that achieving agreement within a nation-state was difficult enough, let alone on a global scale.

**Critiques and Global Extensions of Rawls' Ideas**

Despite the elegance of Rawls' framework, critics like Amartya Sen (1933–present) and Thomas Pogge (1953–present) have argued that limiting justice to national systems is insufficient in an interconnected world. They highlight issues like global poverty, climate change and migration, which transcend national borders and demand international solutions.

**Amartya Sen's Critique:** Sen expanded Rawls' ideas by emphasizing capabilities – what individuals can actually achieve in their lives – over the mere distribution of resources. He argued that global institutions should address inequalities between nations, not just within them. Sen pointed to global health crises, where international cooperation is essential for equitable vaccine distribution, as a challenge to Rawls' domestically focused framework.

**Thomas Pogge's Global Extension:** Pogge adapted Rawlsian principles to advocate for global distributive justice. In *World Poverty and Human Rights* (2002), Pogge criticized affluent nations for perpetuating poverty through exploitative global systems, proposing mechanisms like a global resources dividend to redistribute wealth more equitably.

### Rawls' Impact on Political Philosophy

Despite critiques, Rawls' contributions to political philosophy remain unparalleled, particularly in his development of a systematic, principled framework for justice that has influenced both domestic and global debates.

### Revolutionizing the Discipline

1. **Justice as Fairness as a Foundational Framework:** Rawls introduced a methodical, hypothetical construct – the original position and veil of ignorance – to derive principles of justice. This approach shifted political philosophy from abstract theorizing to rigourous normative analysis and also provided a blueprint for analysing real-world policies, such as affirmative action or progressive taxation, in terms of fairness.

2. **Revitalizing Political Philosophy in the Twentieth Century:** Before Rawls, political philosophy had lost prominence, overshadowed by other branches of philosophy. Rawls' *A Theory of Justice* rekindled interest in normative ethics and social contract theory. It influenced countless political thinkers, including Robert Nozick (1938–2002), Martha Nussbaum (1947–present) and G.A. Cohen (1941–2009).

### Extending Rawls' Ideas to Global Contexts

While Rawls himself did not focus extensively on global justice, his framework inspired subsequent philosophers to adapt his ideas. Philosophers like Charles Beitz and Thomas Pogge used Rawlsian principles to argue for global redistributive justice. Beitz's *Political Theory and International Relations* (1979) applied Rawls' difference principle to the global stage, advocating for the redistribution of wealth and resources between nations.

The creation of global metrics like the Human Development Index (HDI) and the principles underpinning Sustainable Development Goals (SDGs) also reflect Rawlsian ideals of fairness and prioritizing the least advantaged.

### Impact on Democracy and Political Thought

Rawls' insistence on fairness as the foundation of justice profoundly shaped democratic theory. His principles provided a moral defence of liberal democracy by highlighting the protection of equal basic liberties, Rawls reinforced the moral legitimacy of democratic systems. His difference principle offers a robust framework for evaluating the fairness of income distribution and social mobility in democratic societies. Modern policies like universal healthcare and progressive taxation reflect Rawlsian principles of justice, demonstrating their practical relevance in shaping fairer societies.

His emphasis on justice within national systems not only revitalized political philosophy but also set the stage for debates on global justice, inspiring generations of thinkers to explore how his principles might address the challenges of an increasingly interconnected world.

## ANECDOTES

### 1. Collegial Debates with Robert Nozick

Rawls maintained a collegial relationship with Robert Nozick (1938–2002) despite their ideological differences. Nozick's libertarian critique of *A Theory of Justice in Anarchy, State, and*

*Utopia* (1974) sparked one of the most influential philosophical debates of the twentieth century.

These debates elevated both thinkers, showcasing Rawls' ability to engage respectfully with dissenting views. Nozick's criticism forced Rawls to refine his arguments, particularly around the difference principle, further enriching the discourse on political philosophy.

### 2. Writing and Rewriting *A Theory of Justice*

Rawls took over a decade to write *A Theory of Justice*, meticulously revising drafts to address potential critiques. Even after its publication in 1971, he continued to refine the work, particularly in response to feminist and libertarian criticisms.

This iterative process underscores his intellectual integrity and openness to criticism. It highlights his commitment to justice as a collaborative pursuit, reflecting his belief in continuous improvement and inclusivity in philosophical inquiry.

### 3. Mentorship and Legacy at Harvard University

While teaching at Harvard University (1959–91), Rawls mentored many prominent philosophers, including Martha Nussbaum, Thomas Nagel and G.A. Cohen. Known for his humility, Rawls often credited his students with helping him refine his ideas.

His mentorship extended his influence beyond his own works. His students applied and expanded his theories, ensuring that his principles of justice as fairness reached new domains like feminist theory (Nussbaum), ethical philosophy (Nagel) and Marxist critiques (Cohen).

## Why His Ideas Matter Today

John Rawls revolutionized political philosophy by crafting a vision of justice that remains both aspirational and achievable. His framework of justice as fairness, anchored in the concepts of the veil of ignorance and the original position, redefined how societies should think about fairness, equality and moral reasoning. By centering the dignity of the individual and the needs of the least advantaged, Rawls offered a counterpoint to utilitarianism and other traditions that often subordinated individual rights to collective outcomes.

His work stands at the intersection of theory and practice, influencing not only philosophers but also policymakers, educators and activists around the globe. His ideas have become touchstones in debates on healthcare, education, income redistribution and global justice, while his emphasis on fairness resonates with movements for racial and gender equality.

As the final philosopher in this collection, Rawls represents a culmination of the timeless pursuit of justice and moral order. His ideas encapsulate the power of political philosophy to challenge the status quo, provide ethical frameworks and envision societies where fairness and equity prevail. However, his legacy is not confined to his theories; it is an invitation to continually reimagine and strive for a more just world.

While the broader challenges of inequality, climate change, and pluralism remain, his vision serves as a guiding light – a reminder that justice, fairness and equality are not abstract ideals but essential foundations for human flourishing. His work is a testament to the enduring relevance of philosophy as a practical and transformative force, inspiring us to build societies that reflect our highest aspirations.

# 6

# A CALL TO ENGAGE

## *Political Philosophy as a Living Conversation*

So far, we have traced the evolution of political philosophy, exploring the ideas of the greatest thinkers who have shaped our understanding of justice, power, freedom and governance. We examined their lives, their core contributions and the key questions they posed to the world. Now, as we reach the final chapter, let us take a step beyond history. Rather than merely reflecting on what these philosophers have said, imagine them engaged in a conversation, a debate that transcends time, to confront the pressing challenges of our modern world.

The room was grand yet unassuming – a circular chamber lined with towering bookshelves, their spines heavy with the wisdom of centuries. A long wooden table stood at the centre, its surface reflecting the soft glow of candlelight. Six thinkers from across centuries, present as though time itself had folded, took their seats.

Plato, draped in a simple tunic, leaned forward with a serene yet commanding presence. 'What is justice in today's world?' he asked, his voice calm but insistent.

Before he could expand, B.R. Ambedkar straightened in his chair, his expression resolute. 'Justice is not theoretical, Plato. It is lived. It is the dismantling of entrenched hierarchies that deny dignity to millions.'

Thomas Hobbes tapped his fingers on the table. 'Justice is important, yes, but the world is not driven by ideals alone. What of power? What happens when artificial intelligence, unregulated and unchecked, holds dominion over human affairs? It could destabilize society faster than any war.'

From across the table, Hannah Arendt lifted her gaze. 'It is not the machines we should fear, Hobbes, but those who control them. Power lies in the hands of those who shape truth, and when truth is twisted, freedom crumbles.'

John Rawls, ever the architect of fairness, shifted the discussion. 'Then let us ensure AI is governed by justice. Technology should serve the least advantaged, not deepen inequality. Just as in governance, fairness is non-negotiable.'

Friedrich Nietzsche, who had been silent until now, let out a short laugh. 'Fairness? Justice? These are shackles. Power does not serve, it asserts! Let us not forget that creativity and willpower drive innovation, even in chaos.'

The conversation pivoted, drawn now to the planet itself. Arendt sighed. 'What of climate change? If we destroy the world, what good is freedom? The true crisis of our age is not just political – it is existential.'

Plato considered her words and nodded. 'Perhaps only a wise and virtuous leadership – a modern philosopher-king – can steer humanity away from its ruin.'

Ambedkar shook his head firmly. 'No, Plato. The solution cannot come from a single ruler, no matter how wise. The voices of the marginalized must be central, not an afterthought. Justice demands that those most affected lead the way.'

**Imagining a Utopian World**

Yet, a utopia is not merely imagined, it is built through action. And beyond this chamber, in the real world, the echoes of their debate were already shaping lives.

The debate grew into a vision of the future, each thinker shaping a fragment of what could be:

- Plato suggests a global council of ethical leaders to address climate and AI ethics.
- Hobbes warns of potential disorder if such power is unchecked, advocating for strict laws.
- Ambedkar demands that this council represent the oppressed and marginalized, ensuring their voices shape policies.
- Nietzsche pushes back, arguing for bold and creative solutions beyond moral conventions.
- Rawls proposes a 'planetary veil of ignorance', forcing leaders to design policies without knowing their position in society.
- Arendt stresses the need for public accountability, emphasizing that governance cannot exist in secrecy or manipulation.

The utopia remains incomplete, a dynamic and evolving vision – an invitation for you to reimagine reality.

## The Personal Is Political

But philosophy does not remain confined to scholarly debate. It breathes in the struggles of those who shape society through their actions:

- A female scientist, inspired by Arendt, uncovered biases in AI algorithms.
- A grassroots activist, channeling Ambedkar, fought for climate justice in the slums of Mumbai.
- A young philosopher, torn between Plato's ideals and Nietzsche's defiance, questioned societal norms in her conservative hometown.

These are not isolated acts. They reflect a deeper, urgent need for guiding principles in our modern world. And from their debate, a manifesto emerged, an outline for the future of justice, freedom and responsibility.

## A Philosophical Manifesto for the Future

1. Justice must dismantle social, economic and environmental inequities.
2. Freedom must balance innovation with accountability in the age of AI.
3. Truth must remain the foundation of governance, resisting misinformation.
4. Equality must address historical injustices and ensure representation.
5. The climate crisis must be seen as the ultimate test of collective responsibility.
6. Power must serve the common good while fostering individual creativity and diversity.

But philosophy is not built on declarations alone. It is shaped by those who choose to act. And so, the question remains, what role will you play?

### Beyond the Debate: Philosophy in Action

As the conversation drew to a close, Ambedkar rose from his chair. His voice, unwavering, carried across the room.

'What will you do to ensure justice and dignity for those whose voices remain unheard?' Arendt stood beside him, her words measured yet urgent. 'Will you fight to preserve freedom, even when truth is contested?'

And finally, Rawls turned to you, my reader. 'In a world shaped by artificial intelligence and climate crises, how will you choose fairness over convenience?'

The candlelight flickered. The room fell silent. There were no easy answers, only the quiet certainty that political philosophy was still being written.

And the next chapter belonged to those who dared to ask the questions.

# NOTES